LIFE is a
CHALLENGE

Journey *to* Discover *the* Secret to Life

EROL HAFIZBEGOVIC

BALBOA.
PRESS

A DIVISION OF HAY HOUSE

Balboa Press books may be ordered through booksellers or by contacting:

Balboa Press
A Division of Hay House
1663 Liberty Drive
Bloomington, IN 47403
www.balboapress.com
1 (877) 407-4847

Because of the dynamic nature of the Internet, any web addresses or links contained in this book may have changed since publication and may no longer be valid. The views expressed in this work are solely those of the author and do not necessarily reflect the views of the publisher, and the publisher hereby disclaims any responsibility for them.

The author of this book does not dispense medical advice or prescribe the use of any technique as a form of treatment for physical, emotional, or medical problems without the advice of a physician, either directly or indirectly. The intent of the author is only to offer information of a general nature to help you in your quest for emotional and spiritual well-being. In the event you use any of the information in this book for yourself, which is your constitutional right, the author and the publisher assume no responsibility for your actions.

Any people depicted in stock imagery provided by Thinkstock are models, and such images are being used for illustrative purposes only. Certain stock imagery © Thinkstock.

Print information available on the last page.

ISBN: 978-1-5043-4362-6 (sc)
ISBN: 978-1-5043-4364-0 (hc)
ISBN: 978-1-5043-4363-3 (e)

Library of Congress Control Number: 2015917388

Balboa Press rev. date: 10/29/2015

To my dear children,
Leila and Omar

CONTENTS

Introduction ix

Book on Life 1

Book on Religion 80

Book on Wealth 108

Book on Health 124

Book on Death 138

Acknowledgements 149

References 153

INTRODUCTION

"Cogito Ergo Sum" translates into "I think, therefore I am." It is a very popular phrase that proves the existence—and it was written by the French philosopher—Rene Descartes. This legendary philosophical phenomenon was written in his book Principles of Philosophy; in its Latin language version, published in 1644. This proposition became a fundamental element of the Western philosophy—and it was perceived to form a foundation for all knowledge. A very simple phrase, which tells so much. I believe, and hope, that is how you will feel after reading this book; it is written very simple, with a view on life from an average, family orientate person—not a celebrity—but just an ordinary citizen of the world, who traveled to over 25 counties.

For me, it all started back in the eighties. The day was sunny and bright, I was twelve years old. My best friend Vanis, and I, were jumping and walking on some brick walls, which connected some car garages; and at one moment I stepped on a loose brick of the connecting walls. That very old brick was not attached to the wall anymore, because it's old cement had dried out—and I went flying over eight feet to the ground, hitting my head in the process. While I was lying motionless on the ground, my best friend was thinking that I had died.

I had woken up in the hospital asking the nurse "Where am I?" and "Why am I in this bed?" A little while after, my parents and sister walked into the room, and told me what had happened. I was very lucky, because after that big fall, I only had some bruises on my body—and a little bump on my head. Even though my brain suffered a concussion, which is a minor traumatic brain injury that occurred when my head had hit the ground—it was not life threatening. Momentarily, all of that day was erased from my memory, and when the doctor had asked me how old I was, I answered: "Four, of course," even though I was twelve. Luckily, it was temporary memory loss, and most of my memory of that day came back to me, after some time. I was in the hospital for a few days, thinking about different things. That is when I started questioning myself: "I am alive that's great, but what are we people doing here on this earth, what is the purpose of life?" Tough questions to answer, for a twelve year old. The hospital is a place where we can learn a lot about life. We can see a lot of suffering there—and logically start to appreciate life more. Also, we see a lot of hope from friends and family. Hospitals are places where we see who really cares about us, and we realize who our real friends are. The most honest prayers are prayed there, and people pray in different ways to whomever they believe in—and it does not bother anyone. People just want to get better. After I was released from the hospital, I went back to doing the typical things a teenage boy does in his life, like thinking about girls, homework, Commodore 64 games, etc.

It was not till 1992, when the attack on Sarajevo began—and after I had learned that some of my family and friends were killed, I had started asking the same questions to myself; I was sixteen years old at that point. All I was thinking was: "This war is nonsense, good people are dying, why?" And the same questions again: "What is the reason for living this life?" and "What is the meaning of life?" A couple of years before the war my parents had bought me a camcorder, and I actually had taped parts of my life during the war; I did not want to record any dead bodies or blood, just some damage to the buildings—and to document how the life in my city was in between the attacks. Officially, 11541 of my city's residents were unlucky to survive. Thousands of bombshells were thrown onto Sarajevo from surrounding hills, also snipers were killing people daily. Tragically, one lady got killed just a few steps in front of me, by a sniper. I ran back home all shaken up. Another time, I was going to my friend's house, and when I was crossing the street I had noticed a big puddle of blood, one person hidden by a building near me was telling me: "Run, run there was a guy just hit with a sniper bullet." I also experienced a lot of close calls with the explosions of the mortar grenades nearby. Usually, the soldiers that have kept the city under the siege would throw one bombshell grenade into a residential neighborhood—and then they waited for some time until people would come out to see the damage the bombshell had done, or if somebody was wounded. Right after, those soldiers would throw another bombshell, into the same area—to kill even more. Every day it was like a gamble to walk outside a sheltered area; it was a very tough time to live there. Stanislav Galić, soldier and former commander of one branch in the Army of Republika Srpska (Bosnian Serbs Army), was convicted of Terror as a Crime against humanity, and murder as violations of the laws and customs of War. It was proven in court, that he was commanding the attack on the City. For his part in the Siege of Sarajevo, Mr. Galić was sentenced to "twenty years to life," by the International Court for War Crimes in Den Hague, The Netherlands.

My spirit was high during the war, even though I had seen a lot of people being killed, I did not think it was my time yet. I was telling myself: "You are a young guy, and you have your whole life in front of you." It looks like I was right, I survived. The war did take away part of my childhood, but I had learned a huge life lesson; I had learned how to collect energy from the good God. Later in my life I'd read the book Man's Search For Meaning, by Victor E. Frankly—who had survived the Second World War, and imprisonment in concentration camp. He had watched people die every day, and Mr. Frankl noticed that when somebody lost their will for life—those people were usually dead in the next few days. When those poor people would scream: "I cannot take this any longer," they lost will for living the life. Soon-after, they would either get killed by a guard, illness, or sometimes they would just hold onto the electric barb wire—killing themselves instantly. Good thing Mr. Frankl believed in the better days, he survived. That was a great life lesson, which shows if people lose their will for living there is a big chance they will die soon.

I was married young, at the age of 21. I got married in the New York City Hall—to a beautiful, and smart girl with the same family heritage as mine. I was told by many people: "You are too young," I actually had the feeling, that they were thinking it was not going to last. Well, we celebrated our 18 years of marriage—and it's been working well. Keeping a family together is a hard job now-days, I just recently read that almost fifty percent of all marriages end up in divorce; when I see older couples holding hands and smiling, that makes me very happy. During my working days, as a professional luxury taxi driver, I've met thousands and thousands of people—and many of them have made influence on me. Talking about marriage and success in life, I will mention one special individual—Mr. Red McCombs. That gentleman was in Orlando for his granddaughter's wedding, and I was a very lucky guy to be his chauffeur. Amazingly enough, at eighty-something years old he still treats his wife as a princess; I was especially amazed after I had learned later by reading his book, which he mailed it to me, that they are together for over 58 years. I was honestly amazed with their love; they actually still look very much in love. Their story started as a very ordinary American couple, they did not have much in the beginning of their life together. Technically, just with will, and love for family, Mr. McCombs has developed many business—that have put him on the list of the top richest people in the world, by the famous Forbes Magazine. During his best working years, at separate times, he owned: San Antonio Spurs, Denver Nuggets, and Minnesota Vikings. He has tower building named after him, and also he owned one of the biggest Ford dealerships in the world. All those years his strong wife Charlene and he stood together. Having all that money, and power, he could have had many new ladies every year, but he showed strong character, and stayed together with his one true love. I am taking him as a role model of the person who is living meaningful life. After seeing them together, it actually made me love my wife even more.

The greatest moment of my life was when my daughter was born. I was twenty two years old; and I was definitely very happy. For the first couple of weeks after she was born, I stopped every day, on my way from work back home, into one of Manhattan's lower priced stores—to buy her a toy. At that time I had a very low-paying job, and occasionally I would skip lunch, but I had to bring her a toy—every day. I'd felt so proud, like I was the only guy in the whole world who has a kid; I was jumping with joy. When I was 24, my son was born—similar feelings followed for me, as when his sister was born. Many-times, I was holding my dear son in my arms, and I was praying for him and his sister to become good people. Before I had a plan for my life, I was planning there's; wishing for God to put them on the right life's path, to achieve something in their life, and I still do. When I was about 25, and after playing with my babies—I decided to write them some notes about life, and my view on life, which eventually can help them when they grow up. Over the years those notes have evolved into this book idea. Originally, I was going to write mostly of how God had helped me, but over the years, that idea had evolved more into searching for what the meaning of life is. Already before having children I was trying hard to find the meaning to life, and having them gave me even more power and will—to discover it. That is how I've gotten the idea to write this book. Over the last fifteen years I have spent a few hours a day, every single day, thousands and thousands of hours in total. From the original idea to write personal notes for my kids, the new idea was born to write a book not just for my children—but for everyone who is interested in finding our life's purpose.

Many times, over many years, I have transported very important people—as a part of my job. Sometimes, on my paperwork it would say that they are important, but I have never heard of many of them. When I started using Google, it was easier to know who I am driving. One time, one name I was definitely able to recognize without Google—and that was the name of good man—Malcolm Gladwell. I was so excited to pick him up, at one of Disney's hotel; and I am sure, that because of my excitement, I was probably looking very Goofy to him (pun-intended). As a professional chauffeur I am supposed to stay quiet, and only answer to customer's questions, but I was too excited, and had to tell him that I love all of his books—and that I also own them—all but one. When we came to the airport, he handed me a twenty dollar bill as a gratuity, which I tried twice to reject, but he insisted, and I took it. Right away I said: "Okay then, I promise that with this money, I will go and buy your book—the one that I am missing, as soon as possible." Mr. Gladwell answered: "That's a smart investment." In his book Outliers, he predicts, that if you have spent 10,000 hours doing anything, you will become good at it. Well, I have spent well over 10,000 hours thinking, and researching, what is our purpose in this life, and I believe that I am totally ready to write about the subject.

BOOK ON LIFE

1.

Life is the only thing, that we actually own. We have the power to decide, in most cases, what we want to do with it. Sometimes, life experiences can write interesting stories, and I am assured that you—who are reading this, have a story to tell too. I am actually totally free of doubt that we all do. When I moved to New York in 1994, it was impressive to witness the clash of the different cultures in the City. People from all around the world are living together, and most definitely in my opinion—New York City is the best place to learn about life. On the regular basis, I used to buy coffee, and butter rolls—at my favorite NY Deli. Right outside that Deli, there was a man who was spending his days with his back against the wall at all times; it had seemed to me, as if he was living there. He did not speak much, but occasionally, would spare a smile—revealing the presence of a good soul inside of him. A friend of mine told me his story once, that at one point of that man's life, he was living the good and happy life. His family had moved to America from India, where they were of the higher social status. That gentleman was too weak towards alcohol, and even though he failed in his life; he would still have an interesting story to write. Again, I am pretty sure that every single living human, has a story to tell; from the homeless guy you walk by on the street to the taxi driver, from your fitness instructor to your favorite store owner—absolutely everyone, including you again, of course.

2.

What is life? Does life have any meaning? Once we become aware of the inner feeling, that feeling inside of our mind, of rightness or wrongness of our behavior, we can start actually living. Usually something has to shake us up, to wake us up—from taking life for granted. I think, that life is a reward, and we should consider ourselves lucky and awarded—many people never realize that. There is not a single day that I spend without being aware, that I am alive; and that really makes me happy. Every single day I learn something new, and thanks to my life's experiences I have that story to tell. During our lifetime we make choices, choices which shape our life, sometimes for the better, and sometimes for the worse. Our deeds are the only thing we will leave behind us, when we die. When we become fully aware of our life we can start living the good life. Logically, the more good things we complete during our lifetime the better, of course; but even knowing this many times people knowingly do the wrong things. What I have learned during my life thus far, is that old proverb "what goes around comes around" is extremely true—and everybody will have to deal with the results of the actions they have taken during their lifetime.

3.

I have realized during my journey to find my purpose in life, that it is the purpose that I need to give to my life; thereafter in my search for the meaning, I have learned that, "Your purpose in life is to find your purpose and give your whole heart and soul to it," which was told a very long time ago—by Buddha. Don't jump on the conclusion right away that I am a Buddhist, because I am not;

still, later in this book I will mention Buddha just as the one of my greatest teachers. If we search hard enough, and involve our full potential, we can find most of the answers—for the things that we are looking for, within ourselves. Sometimes answers are so simple, and are around us all of the time, but we do not proceed to obtain knowledge. Our own life experience, together with the information which we have gained from the books we have read, is precious in obtaining the knowledge. I was shot at during the war in Bosnia, where I grew up. A few times I had heard sniper bullets hitting the ground near me, and so many grenades exploded in my vicinity. Sounds of flying shrapnel's from grenades sounded like whistling screams—just hearing them left a large scar on my brain. That sound has been memorized in my mind, and ever since I have felt uncomfortable hearing any loud noise. Recently, there was this driver in the car right in front of me, at a traffic light—he did not want to move his car when the green arrow was telling him he could go—after I had confronted him, he pulled out a hand gun on me. I was not scared, I even continued talking to him "for that you can go to prison," I told him. His answer was: "This is Florida." Valuing my life I just drove off. There are so many vicious people in the world that have no respect of life. I have many different experiences in my life, and I have learned to value this precious life that I have. My favorite Roman Emperor Marcus Aurelius wrote in his book Meditations: "When you arise in the morning think of what a privilege it is to be alive, to think, to enjoy, to love." Being very close to dangerous situations in my life a few times, I am even more grateful for every new day I live.

4.

Most of my adult life I have worked as a professional luxury vehicle chauffeur, and by doing my job I have transported probably around a hundred thousand individuals. On a regular basis, I talk to many customers, and many customers have talked back to me; they gave me the power to listen, and to learn. People in general are nice, and quite a few of my customers became my friends. In total, I have heard many interesting stories. Of course some people did not talk, but many did—and being very social, I listened to their stories. One of my favorite philosophers, Confucius had said, that, "You cannot open the book without learning something," remarkably enough, driving people, and engaging into interesting conversations, I have learned something new, every single day. As I said, in my opinion, except personal experience, most things I have learned I owe to the teachers, that wrote the books I have read—which I have studied for hundreds, or maybe even thousands of hours. The amazing thing to me is, that many of these great books were written very many years ago, and still have a powerful meaning. My conclusion is that the best teachers handed down the knowledge that we seek, and the only thing we need to do is to combine it with personal experience; that is the way to find the answer to what the meaning of our life is, what is our purpose, and what is the secret to life; the hardest questions ever, for all philosophers, and I truly wonder sometimes, if everyone will ever agree on the exact same answer. Regardless, if everyone will agree on the same answer or not, we still have to try hard to acquire certain conclusions.

5.

I find it very interesting that most people I transport do not think deep into their life. Most everybody is into their day to day problems. With very few, I have involved myself into the conversation about what I think is going to happen to the world. Those people were usually very eager to hear the stories that I loved to talk about, about world extinction. I would start explaining how it is easy to figure out that we humans are just temporary inhabitants of the Earth. Our own human life span average is fifty to eighty years, depending how we live our life—and where we live, on this planet. Looking at the larger picture, the whole human life is still just an episode in the history of our world, that we call Earth. We have to make it worth remembering episode. Thanks to science, now we know that about 4.54 billion years ago primordial earth had been formed, from the cosmic dust, particles of ice, and gases. In the whole Universe, which thanks to the Wilkinson Microwave Anisotropy Probe of NASA, we know is 13.772±0.059 billion years old, the Earth is the only known place that can harbor life. There is evidence that goes back to 3.5 billion years ago of the first ever existing life form, in the structure of microbial mat-fossils found in 3.48 billion year old sandstone. The minuscule remains of those single-celled microbes were discovered in Australia, by the scientist from Old Dominium University located in the U.S. Those microbes are possible ancestors to all species, including humans. In the last 3.5 billion years a great number of species have lived on Earth—but is believed that 99 percent of them are estimated to be extinct, in their original form, by now. The number of current species occupying our planet ranges from 8 million to 14 million, scientists believe; and only about 1.2 million have been documented.

6.

One particular time I had a very long, and interesting conversation with a customer, who must have been a professor; but with me trying to remember all of the details he said, had forgotten to ask him if he was. By that time I had already read a lot about Homo sapiens, but that day I had learned something very interesting about us, anatomically modern humans. It is interesting that Homo sapiens have been living on the Earth for only about 0.2 million years; which looking at the timescale of 3.5 billion years of life on Earth is just like the blink of an eye. We are the only surviving species in the genus of hominids; all others—including archaic humans, became extinct. After agreeing on that information, this customer had proceeded to tell me another interesting fact; him being Caucasian male, that information sounded very honest—he said: "When Homo sapiens left Africa between 40,000 to 200,000 thousand years ago they were dark in skin color, and possibly because of the much different weather up north there was a mutation of one gene MC1R, which regulates melanin, that single gene mutation started the Caucasian race." At that time I did not have access to the Internet in my car—so, I was anxious to get home to search about the gene MC1R. It was a great teaching lesson, which I have received, from that gentleman.

7.

As we've seen in all these numbers mentioned above, there was life long before, and there will be long after humans on Earth disappear. As a matter of fact—our Sun, which is average to small size star in the Milky Way Galaxy, and lies close to the inner rim out of galaxy's Orion arm—has burned its fuel half way through. It is calculated, that the Sun's orbit around the Milky Way is elliptical due to the galactic spiral arms. It takes our Solar System about 225–250 million years to complete one orbit through the Milky Way—that is called a Galactic year, thus according to that calculation, the Sun has completed 20–25 orbits during its lifetime.

8.

The Sun is approximately 4.57 billion years old, and there has not been any significant changes in the last four billion years. Ones however, when hydrogen fusion in its core stops, the Sun will undergo severe changes, and will become a red giant; as soon as it happens, most likely, a newly shaped star is going to swallow the nearest three planets, which are Mercury, Venus, and Earth first. Our star oscillates up and down relative to the galactic plane, approximately 2.7 times per orbit; so, while the Sun is orbiting around the Milky Way, it is a quite possible when it goes through the higher density spiral arms, it can coincide with mass extinction on Earth.

9.

Jack J. Sepkoski and David M. Raup identified, and well documented, five mass extinctions of living life on Earth—and they published their work in 1982. Since then, a lot of authors and enthusiasts have called it the Big Five extinctions. Here they are, all five, mentioned in a few words: Extinction that happened the farthest from our time was Ordovician-Silurian extinction event, which was between 440 and 450 million years ago. At that time 27% of all the families, 57% of all genera and 60% to 70% of all species were killed. The second farthest event was the Late Devonian extinction that was happening between 360 and 375 million years ago. It had eliminated about 19% of all families, 50% of all genera and 70% of all the species. Third in line was Permian-Triassic extinction event, that happened approximately 251 million years ago, and was so devastating that wiped 57% of all families, 83% of all genera, and about 90% to 96% of all species on the face of the Earth. That is about 96% of all marine species, and an estimated 70% of land species. The second closest extinction event to our time was Triassic-Jurassic extinction event that happened 200 million years ago. About 23% of all families, 48% of all genera (20% of marine families and 55% of marine genera), and 70% to 75% of all species became extinct. Most non-dinosaurian archosaurus, most therapsids, and most of the large amphibians were dead—leaving dinosaurs with little competitions on land, while diapsids dominated the marine life. The closest to our time was Cretaceous-Paleocene extinction event that happened about 66 million years ago. Most people are very familiar with this one, for the reason that all non-avian dinosaurs were wiped out from the face of the Earth. Altogether, when this event happened about 17% of all the families, 50% of all genera and 75% of all the species became extinct. It drastically reduced the life in the seas, and on the land too. Mammals and birds became dominant land vertebrates at that time.

10.

As I've mentioned above, our Sun is a star—and there are billions of stars just in our cluster of stars, that we call Milky Way. There are billions, and billions of galaxies, like the Milky Way; some galaxies are smaller than ours, and some much bigger—in the Universe that we share. All of the galaxies also have billions of stars just like our Sun. Trying to count how many stars are in the Universe, combining all the galaxies, is an impossible task. The reason for this conclusion is because the number of stars may not have an end; it could go on to infinity. Even if there was an end to our Universe, then the question would be, what comes after that? Maybe, there are other Universes out there, in addition to ours. Possibly our whole Universe is just like the atom size, in comparison to some unknown super Universe. The question then again is, what is after that? Regardless, the number of stars in the already known Universe is so high, that it is difficult for our brains to imagine. Many of this, possibly infinite number of stars have multiple planets—so overall, it is possible, that somewhere out there is a planet with intelligent lifeforms—possibly as beautiful as our own—jewel planet Earth.

11.

To sustain living organisms, and life in general, the planet has to be perfectly positioned toward its Sun. For example, if the Earth was just a minuscule distance closer, or farther, from the Sun, life as we know it would have been wiped out. The reason for that is because it would be either too hot, or too cold to harbor life. I always find great pleasure in watching NASA videos from the International Space Station, which by the way is not too far from the Earth. It is orbiting around the Earth on an average distance between 205 and 270 miles. That distance is approximately like the driving distance between New York and Boston, just go from NY into the sky instead of to Boston—which in space travel is a trivial distance. Still, it is far enough, to gives us pictures, and videos of our marble looking beautiful planet. We are so lucky, because looking at the vast darkness of the Universe, it looks like we are living in Heaven. Actually, when we ask people how they imagine Heaven, they would usually explain it like some beautiful place that we already have here on Earth. Hey, maybe we are all in Heaven already. Hmmmm.

12.

Imagine now, we are standing on the outskirts of one average to small planet, orbiting an average to small star, in the average to small Galaxy. Definitely by now you are getting the idea that we are not in the center of the Universe. Every day, I encounter people that think they are ruling the worlds, and they believe they are in the center of the Universe—oblivious of the reality, they most definitely think that the Universe revolves around them; and also without a doubt they believe, deep inside, to be the smartest. This happens because they never thought of the larger picture, as shown above. Do you really think that God, the Creator of the Universe, would send his son to die on some undeveloped, unnoticed smaller planet. Especially, to die for the sins of all inhabitants of the Universe. With all due respect, I do love Jesus Christ; and I think that he was a good man, who had tried everything to help people—and in his short life he had left great legacy, but there is no way that he is God, which technically he would be if he was Son of God. I believe, somewhere out there, in the vast space of the Universe, there is a ruling Universal Energy—the Energy that can influence all of the things in the whole Universe, not just things on the microscopic size planet Earth. Well, it is microscopic in comparison to the rest of Universe, of course. That Energy is influencing absolutely everything in the Universe, including us as well—because we are a part of it. We, and the whole Universe—are under that Energy's control. The whole Universe, and all the Stars of course, contain chemical elements like carbon, oxygen, hydrogen, and nitrogen, which are also indispensable for life on Earth, and our bodies too. As the thirteenth century Persian poet Rumi wrote in one of his songs: "I am dust particles in sunlight," which definitely makes clear sense. In the full picture of the Universe, people are smaller than the smallest atom, looking on the atoms here on Earth—but we are still part of Mother Universe. We are all connected—but we still have to follow ethical rules to give meaning to our life. That Universal Energy I call Dear God, and yes, it is one God for all of us. I will explain myself more in the religion part of this book.

13.

Coming back to the extinction story, I am sure you have already figured out what I meant by saying earlier, that the Human race is just an episode in the history of the World. It is only a question of time when we will be extinct, as well. Even if we find a way to inhabit Mars, which has the same Sun as the Earth, that only would prolong extinction for a little while. As of today, I don't think that we humans, at the moment, even have technology to land Spacecraft with people on to the Moon, by the way which is very close in space travel, being only 238,900 miles away from Earth. Mentioning that, imagine then; how long it would take us to safely fly and land a Spacecraft, with a crew, on Mars, which is on average 140,000,000 miles away? Imagine then, how long it would take us to fly to the other Stars? I will come back to that little bit later.

14.

There are a few possible future extinctions story scenarios. Same as with earlier extinctions, it would be rapid, and a widespread decrease in the amount of life on Earth. It would have to be something similar to the big five extinction to be able to wipe out all the humans; which by the way we would not have control of. More likely, human species face partly extinction in near future, possibly of its own negligibility. There are so many different extinction scenarios talked about in the popular culture, science, science fiction, and of course religion. The extinction, or the partly extinction, we humans would be guilty of, is if we start a global nuclear war—or if some, out of mind individual, or country, would release a deadly virus. There is also a huge threat from the causes we humans do towards global warming.

15.

Because of our industrial expansion, we humans release too high of an amount of deadly gases into the ozone—as we all know that increases global warming. Imagine this: Earth gets much warmer, a couple of the Super-volcanos on the Earth can get very hot, and erupt. That eruption would send tons and tons of deadly ash, and vapor into the sky. In the short time—that huge ash cloud would block sunlight, and we would witness a chain reaction; it would technically, without sunlight for an extended period of time, trigger a small Ice Age. Soon after, plants would start dying, for the reason that they also need the sunlight for photosynthesis, in a process to convert light energy from the Sun into chemical energy. Acid rain would start falling— because volcanos would release toxic gases, such as carbon dioxide, sulfur dioxide, hydrogen sulfide, carbon monoxide, etc. With the blocked sunlight, and constant acid rainfall—famines and a scarcity of drinking water would follow. Without sunlight, it would get very cold in affected areas. Even if someone have stocked large quantities of food and water, chances are that they will still possibly run out of all of it before Earth would rejuvenate. All flora and fauna of the affected areas would be at verge of extinction. Talking about Super-volcanos, let me mention—that there is one right here in the U.S., in Yellowstone National Park; it is a huge volcanic caldera located underground, hence all the hot springs in the area. If Yellowstone erupts, which one day it will, the results will be totally devastating.

16.

Over the long history of humans inhabiting the Earth, there were many terrible epidemics of infectious diseases. A whole separate book can be written on that subject, so I'll just mention a few, to give you an idea. Those are not necessarily human extinction events, but would cause huge damage in a number of human lives. One of the most devastating pandemics in human history was the Black Death plague; it is estimated that at least 75 million people in the world died from it. The high estimate is up to 200 million. Considering, that in those years in the middle of the fourteenth century world population was estimated to be about 450 million—it tells us—that the world have lost approximately from 15% to 40% of its human inhabitants.

17.

In 1918, news came from Spain of a grave illness. It was an unusually deadly influenza pandemic, that have infected many people in the countries across the world, including the Arctic, and very remote islands in the Pacific. Because information about this influenza came from Spain first, it is now known as the Spanish flu. It is really amazing how quickly it had spread across the whole world. That influenza had proved, that even though we think that Earth is very large, we are still all connected, as the deadly virus most likely flew with the wind. The bottom line is, that about 500 million people were infected—and an estimate is that 50 to 100 million died from this terrible pandemic.

18.

When I was maybe 7 or 8 years old, my family went to the movie theater to see the motion picture Variola Vera, which was based on the true story of the 1972 smallpox outbreak in Yugoslavia; that was the country I was living in at that time. It was so scary, that movie probably made changes on my brain, because even now as a grown man I have chills when just thinking about those scenes of infected people with smallpox. Later, I had learned that actually 35 people have died from that particular outbreak, which was, by the way, the last one in Europe—thus far. A disease similar or the same to smallpox, known as Antonine Plague, had in the mid second century killed approximately 30% of all residents in Europe, Western Asia, and Northern Africa. According to CNN, just as recent as 2012, approximately 122,000 people worldwide died from measles—a highly contagious disease caused by a virus. Also Typhoid fever still kills around 216,000 people per year. Tuberculosis, an infectious bacterial disease, killed an estimated 1.3 million in 2012. That shows that even now, in the twenty first century, many people are still dying from the old world diseases.

19.

Many countries have different samples of the viruses in their stock, mostly for educational purposes. It is very scary to think about, what if those viruses would get into the hands of somebody who would be willing to release it. Again, maybe that would not wipe all life on Earth, but it would definitely make devastating damage. Just think of the idea of how deadly, viruses can be; I will take for example the infectious viruses—that have been spreading in the New World explained in the book The Columbian Exchange, written in 1972 by Alfred Crosby—an American historian. His book explains that in between the other things, Europeans exchanged also many illnesses, and viruses with native people of America; it all started happening with Christopher Columbus coming to the New World in 1492. Mr. Crosby explained that people in the New World were introduced with smallpox, measles, yellow fever, influenza, and chicken pox by Europeans. On the other side, he believed that natives transferred syphilis, polio, hepatitis, and encephalitis to Europeans. Native people suffered a much larger loss, due to the devastating power of smallpox disease. A similar thing also had happened in Central and South America with the native people of that area—when Europeans arrived. That had showed us, how the world population can be decreased drastically by viruses; but still life on Earth was not wiped out. Some people have natural antibodies, in their bodies that make them resistant to certain viruses.

20.

All of these scary stories of hypothesized end of the human species make us think, right away, of the plan we would need to have in order to protect the lives of our families, and our own. It is good to be prepared at any time. Many countries have secret underground facilities, just for that reason—to hide in case of pandemics breaking out or natural disasters occurring. The only thing is, that the average person most likely would not be allowed to use those underground tunnels and facilities; that's why many individuals have built their own deep cellars, and have them stocked with a large supply of water, food, air purifiers, weapons, fuel, etc. As I said before, it can help temporarily—and in a case of a smaller accident in their part of the world, it can directly save their life. If they would have stayed unprepared, without any shield even a small nuclear, or a natural disaster, would have killed them, most-likely. In the case of the viruses, even though they are transmissible through the air, by being in the isolated area with an air filter you would have most likely saved your life. You would have to make sure not to be in direct contact with the infected, and your shelter must have good air filters—to keep the air clean.

21.

Another threat to human existence is overpopulation. Now at the early 21st century we have already crossed the mark of seven billion people living on this Earth. Just to draw a clearer picture, according to Population Reference Bureau, it was not till the early 19th century that the Earth was inhabited with only one billion people; not to mention that in the time of Jesus Christ there was only about three hundred million people living on the Earth. Many different factors influenced the rapid growth of six billion world inhabitants in just about two centuries. Humans advanced in the science of medicine and industrialization—which was followed with a mass production of food etc. As of now, we still have enough resources of drinking water, and food, to live comfortably in most parts of the world.

22.

Soon, if we continue with the recent rapid increase our human population will face major problems, maybe even in the near future. It is estimated, that under existing conditions Earth has resources to accommodate between 8 and 16 billion people. In 2011 the United Nations estimated that by the year 2050 the world might have 9.3 billion living people, and by the year 2100 most likely just over 10 billion. Overpopulation will bring an increased demand for natural resources, such as fossil fuels, and again fresh water, and food. All of that in the near future can trigger resource wars, which might be happening already.

23.

Talking about rapid population increase, I'll take one country as an example—India. It is estimated that in the 19th century India's population was a little over 100 million residents, and now there are over 1.2 billion people living there. That is over 17.5% of the world population, and keep in mind that India, even being a huge country, only occupies 2.4% of the world's land. There are more people living there—then in all of the African continent, as of now. The question is if they will have enough of a supply of drinking water, food, and infrastructure, in the near future, if they continue at the same growth rate, as in the last two hundred years. That country enriched the world so many large thinkers, and extraordinary people of significant importance. We need it to be safe; well, we need all of the countries to be safe, as well.

24.

I have one more thing I would like to mention about pandemics. Viruses mostly attack humans, and only a few other living organisms. I am saying this to clarify a difference between human extinction, and the extinction of all life on Earth. Some new pandemics can almost eliminate humanity—while the rest of life would continue their business as usual. In the case of ecological collapse, ecosystems would suffers drastically, and most likely permanent damage to all living organisms; if that happens, then it would be considered to be a mass extinction.

25.

I am leaving the last extinction story scenario to a massive comet, or asteroid impact on Earth. The last one of the five extinction events happened like this, as it is widely believed, when asteroid had hit the Earth in the Gulf of Mexico, 65 to 66 million years ago. That location now is called the Chicxulub crater, and it is about 110 miles wide. The asteroid that had hit that area is estimated to be at least six miles in diameter. The devastation and impact was outstanding, as I mentioned earlier how many species were extinguished. The world's space agencies are constantly scanning the sky for any unexpected meteors, comets, or asteroids for the possible threat of our safety in the near future. As of now there are a few objects that are flying at high speed in our solar system, but luckily none are aiming directly towards the Earth.

26.

I will now come back to the escape to space plan. Even if we succeed to bring manned missions to Mars, and try to colonize it—which is an extraordinary task—Mars is still in our Solar system, as I have said before. Being one of the neighboring planets, Mars is orbiting the same Sun as Earth; and it would have the same faith as Earth, because don't forget our Sun is half way through its life. After our Sun burns all of its fuel, for the next few million years, it will expand into a red giant, burning away its outer layers. That core will form a white dwarf, which is a dense ball of carbon and oxygen. The outcome for that is that the Sun would not be able to produce nuclear energy any longer, but it would still shine, because it would stay very hot. Slowly after that, it would get colder, and finally would match the temperature of the Universe. Our Sun will not end up in a Supernova, or become a Black Hole, simply because it does not have enough mass, as a matter of fact—it would have to be ten times bigger in size—hence I said earlier, our Sun is an average to small in size, compared to the other stars in the Universe. And again, in my opinion, the idea of colonizing Mars is just a temporary solution; anyway, we are still pretty far from the possibility of colonizing it.

27.

That brings me back to the Interstellar travel story—that I have mentioned as the option before. I've heard people talking, "oh, well we will just go to the other stars, and try to inhabit their planets." Let me make this clear—the closest star to our Sun is Proxima Centauri, which is part of Alpha Centauri star system, and it is on average 4.22 to 4.35 million light years away. Just to be clear again—a light year is a distance of approximately 5.88 trillion miles, not million or billion, but trillion, indeed. A light year is the distance that light travels in the vacuum, in one Julian calendar year. Remember, the speed of light is approximately 186,000 miles per second. Remembering the distance from here to the Moon, which is 238,900 mile; that means, we would need technology that would bring an object from Earth to the Moon in approximately 1.3 seconds. Our brain cannot even clearly understand that kind of speed; for example, Voyager 1 is traveling now at the speed level of around 38,000 miles per hour. If Voyager 1 would be traveling into the direction of Alpha Centauri, it would reach it there in about 75,000 years—by that time Alpha Centauri would already be moving away from our Sun, and Voyager 1 would possibly just end up watching how it recedes into the distance. As a reminder, don't forget that Homo Sapiens are inhabiting the Earth for 200,000 years—only. Also, keep in the mind, that Voyager 1 does not have any passengers, and that the fastest manned crew space craft was Apollo 10—returning from the Moon in 1969, it had reached the speed of 24,791 miles per hour—so, even if it had enough fuel, and flew top speed the whole time, it would take a rocket like

Apollo 10 over 100,000 years—just to reach the closest star system to our Sun. Same as with Voyager 1, by the time it would get there—the Alpha Centauri would have receded already farther into space. For a moment I was trying to calculate how many generations of flight crew would have to be born in space, but then I just gave up—way too many.

28.

The interstellar travel idea is pretty old, and in recent history there were many different projects, from many different country's governments, to try to build a spaceship capable of flying beyond our solar system. In this book I decided to mention just a few, that sounded the most interesting. In 1947, Stanislaw Ulam suggested to try nuclear pulse propulsion, a hypothetical method of spacecraft propulsion, that would use nuclear explosions for thrust; which is reaction force described quantitatively by the great Isaac Newton's second and third laws. The idea has evolved into Project Orion— where it was considered that the spacecraft would be directly propelled by a series of atomic bombs explosions, right behind the spacecraft. It would reach the speeds of about 12 times that of the Space Shuttle's main engine. That Project was pretty much over in 1963, when governments of the United States, United Kingdom, and Soviet Union signed the Limited Test Ban Treaty, which was prohibiting all test detonations of nuclear weapons—except if it is underground. Luckily I would think, because who knows what would happen if we continued making nuclear explosions on the Earth. Also it was predicted, that takeoff could have caused premature death of a few crew members—otherwise it had a chance to succeed.

29.

Another Project to try to make a very fast Spacecraft was named Daedalus, which was also a study—as the Project Orion. It was conducted between 1973 and 1978, by the British Interplanetary Society. The plan was to design a plausible interstellar spacecraft, that could reach Alpha Centauri in roughly 45 years; resulting in a velocity of about 10 percent of the speed of light. The spacecraft was going to be fueled by inertial confinement fusion, which in theory uses hot plasma as a fuel; but is pretty much beyond human technical capabilities.

30.

In 1960, physicist Robert Bussard proposed a method of space propulsion—that might have been capable of advanced interstellar spaceflight. This method would use enormous electromagnetic fields to collect, and compress hydrogen from interstellar space. Theoretically, that high speed force would turn mass into a progressively constricted magnetic field—which then directs the energy as rocket exhaust. In this case the Spacecraft would need to be hundreds of kilometers across—just to allow enough hydrogen atoms to funnel through to the reactor. Also, at ship speeds close to the speed of light, Bussard proposed ionizing these atoms—so the cosmic rays would not burn the passengers. Even if this idea would work out, and the Spacecraft left Earth for other stars at this high speed, it would reach it—but as suggested by astronomer Carl Sagan, and many science fiction writers, millions of years would have passed for those left on Earth—just in the case the spaceships' crew would plan to return.

31.

While all of these space travel projects have a chance for success, in a distant future—if we discover new ways to fuel spacecraft. In my personal opinion—chances are very slim for that to happen in my lifetime. There is another idea of space travel proposed trough wormholes. To me, that idea is plain simple Science fiction—but that again, it is just my personal opinion. Well, I hope that physicists will prove me being wrong—one day. To be clear, I wish there was a way to inhabit other star's planets, any possible way; just plain idea of Spacecraft, with a human crew, passing through a wormhole—makes me dizzy. I am still leaving the possibility for that to happen, just because the general theory of relativity published by the genius Albert Einstein in 1915 supports it, and also my favorite physicists Stephen Hawking, and Michio Kaku (who I've met, and talked to), think it is plausible.

32.

The question is now, if we Homo sapiens are here on Earth just temporarily, because our extinction is eminent—is it worth it to leave the legacy? The answer is YES, of course. We may possibly still live on the Earth for thousands of years to come. If the great human minds did not leave written records—we would have had hard time figuring out all of the things we know now about history. As a matter of fact, we segregate history and prehistory—following the invention of writing skills. From the time when anatomically modern humans appeared, some 200,000 years ago, as mention earlier, all the way until the first written documents have appeared—we call that prehistory. Everything after the invention of the writing skills we call modern history. Since the introduction of writing differs from region to region, the beginning of history for different regions differ as well.

33.

Even during Paleolithic times, which name was coined by archaeologist John Lubbock—in his 1872 book Pre-Historic Times, and now commonly called the Stone Age—hominins left recorded marks of their existence on Earth. The Paleolithic Era latest from the first evidence of hominins using stone tools approximately 2.6 million years ago until about 10,000 years before present times—depending again from region to region. For us, the Middle Paleolithic Age is very important, because it had started about 200,000 years ago, the same as when us, Homo Sapiens, emerged. During that time early art had started developing; which we would never have found about, if those hominins did not leave the record behind. The most common form of the art from that time period are paintings—mostly found on the cave's walls. There are also many Paleolithic engravings, Venus figurines, and Paleolithic rock art that have been found all across the world. That shows that leaving legacy behind is the key.

34.

There are many sites in the world that have very well preserved Stone Age art. The list is so large, that again a whole book could be written about it. Here I will mention just a couple: Since I was a school kid, Lascaux cave, located in France—captured my interest. It contains paintings that are estimated to be possibly over 17,000 years old. Beautiful images of large animals are painted so nicely that it is fascinating. Some of those animals, our ancestors painted on the cave walls, are known to be living in that area; we know that from the fossil evidence—and some still live in the same area today. Since it was discovered in 1940, it took some time for people to realize that having too many visitors, with presence of light, carbon dioxide, humidity, germs and bacteria can damage the art. After mold accumulated on the cave walls, it had to be closed for visitors. It is still possible to see how the art looks like, since the replica cave was built nearby. Chauvet cave is also located in France—and it was discovered in 1994, and this cave art is possibly 32,000 years old; it is definitely priceless collection of the prehistoric art, indeed. Authorities worrying of possible damage, rightfully does not allow any visitors, but again there is a replica of the Chauvet cave too. Many other countries including Spain, Morocco, Turkey and Australia—also have the sites with prehistoric art. The good thing is—that the United Nations are preserving many sites through UNESCO (United Nations Educational, Scientific and Cultural Organization). That organization has a monetary fund that, if the site is recognized as a World Heritage Site—it would possibly finance its preservation.

35.

In those Middle Stone Age years, Homo Sapiens coexisted with Homo Erectus, and Neanderthals. It took many years before Homo Sapiens emerged as the only hominin group in Homo genus—to stay alive. It is believed, that approximately seventy thousand years ago the explosion of the Super-volcano Toba, located in present day Lake Toba, Indonesia—made a huge impact on the species within the Homo genus. It is estimated, that approximately 10 to 15 thousand hominins survived the eruption; also possibly that event has influenced Homo Sapiens to leave Africa—because they had left just around that time. Most art found around the world is connected to the Homo Sapiens, even though some very basic prehistoric art can be associated to Homo Erectus, and to Neanderthal figurative art.

36.

Long before any writing systems were developed, it is believed that speech started developing, maybe even five hundred thousand years ago. That was observed through the evolution of the jaw. Studying of anatomic changes in Homo species' sculls during Middle Paleolithic era leaves room for the possibility of modern language capacity. If some form of the speech had been developed during the Paleolithic time—it would be possible that some sort of the music art was introduced too. Without any hard evidence it stays to be just a theory. That's why, leaving hard evidence is the key of the legacy.

37.

During the Neolithic era, which is sometimes called the New Stone Age, which started about 10 to 12 thousand years ago, the earliest forms of the writing have been introduced. Even though counting, and some form of writing numbers, had been in use even during the Paleolithic times—it was not developed into actual writing until about the fourth millennium before the common era, when the Bronze age emerged. Counting was necessary, because in that era, humans started owning some valuable possessions. At those times humans also started domesticating animals, and using of the crops was established. It is believed, that fingers were used first to count the possessions; but as the possession have increased humans invented tallies, as a method for counting. Writing tallies differ from region to region—but placing lines is accepted, as the most common. Usually wood, stone, or bones were used to draw up tally counts.

38.

The Neolithic period was the most important for life as we know it today. At that time people have started living together; they have started forming the settlements, which many of the ruins we have discovered in the last couple of hundreds of years. People then started shifting from—hunting only—to farming, and cultivation. Many wild animals were domesticated during that time. One thing that is very important, and has shaped all the things in the future, was the introduction of writing. As I mentioned earlier, modern history is being counted from the time writing was introduced. There are few different originations of writing stories that exist, but it has been widely accepted that it have started independently—in a few different parts of the world.

39.

There are many records of the writing in the fourth millennium BCE, especially in the area of the Mesopotamia and Egypt. It is believed, that the writing system was first introduced in the Mesopotamia— and not long after that it had reached ancient Egypt. There are quite a few people, which think that Egypt developed writing independently, and maybe even earlier then Mesopotamia—but I will not go further into it. That was the time when the world had been transforming from Neolithic to early Bronze Age. Probably, also totally independent, writing was introduced in China, as it is believed around year 1200 before Christ. Mesoamerica discovered writing around 600 years after China. It is believed again, that their writing system was developed independently too. That new knowledge about the past, and the new way of recording, and keeping track of the things happening in their part of the world, left us the foundation to be able to learn. That foundation is helping us now to know that leaving a legacy is the most important. Those first writers in the Mesopotamia have told us about the events, that have happened even earlier then their time. As said earlier, with the writing History begins. For the areas of the world that waited longer to adopt writing, it took longer to start developing, and were still living in the prehistory.

40.

There were many human settlements on the Earth at the Neolithic era. We are still finding many Neolithic settlement ruins, especially throughout Europe. Those first human settlements had started developing symbol systems to transmit the information; it was pretty simple, and was just for their group use. Appearance of writing due to the cultural diffusion, which people in Mesopotamia used to represent language by using the writing, has developed a whole new civilization of highly intelligent humans. It was obvious, that the Mesopotamians wanted to leave a lasting record. The new system has allowed them to perform better trade, and to be more recognized. That system has allowed their area to bloom, and rightfully to be called the Cradle of the Civilization.

41.

That new system discovered by the Mesopotamians, was the writing of the linguistic symbols to transmit, and to conserve the information. The first form of the writing was logographic in the nature. The logographs were uses to transform plurality of the spoken language; to represent the words with the similar meaning. Logographs represented the words through the graphemes. It is interesting, that over the years our languages have evolved a lot, but we still use the logographer's writing now-days. An example is that every time you are at the mall, or let's say at the airport—you have to follow logographs when you are looking for a toilet, or the ground transportation—in the form of person logograph, or the car logograph.

42.

Sometime later, syllabic, and alphabetic writing had emerged. They are all similar in nature to the logographs, because they also use the grapheme, which is the smallest unit to express the spoken language. For example, the graphemes include Chinese characters, numerical digits, alphabetic letters, the Egyptian hieroglyphs also constitute a variable set of graphemes, etc. So, the most writing systems in general are divided in those three categories—that is logographic, syllabic, and alphabetic writing systems. After the logographs, the syllables appeared as building blocks of the whole words. The syllabic writing system had started a few hundred years before the first alphabetic letters were invented. Even though, Mayan, Akkadian, Chinese, and Sumerian scripts are considered syllabic in nature, they are all still based on the logographs. The latest of all—alphabet systems have emerged, and in that writing system—this book is being written. The alphabet is the standard set of letters to interpret the spoken language. Those letters represent the phonemes, with the basic significant sound. It is considered, that the Phoenician script was the first phonemic script. So, according to that, the Phoenician script is the ancestor of all modern alphabets, like the Latin, Arabic, Greek, Cyrillic, Hebrew, etc. The Greek alphabet has been considered to be the first modern alphabet. The name alphabet comes from the first two letters of the Greek alphabet, Alpha and Beta.

43.

Coming back to the Mesopotamians, and their marvelous idea to make characters in moist clay; which was baked and made possible to last for a long time. They had first used it to trade, to record things being traded, and then they took it to the next level; they had started recording the proverbs, hymns and essays—as a matter of fact, they had started writing, for me, the real history. Individuals were able to write great stories, which were probably known for a long time, through verbal interpretations.

44.

Some of the clay tablets survived to the modern times. Now in the 21st century, I find it a big pleasure to read Sumerian short stories—like: The Debate between Bird and Fish, which had been written over four thousand years ago. One of the original "Great Flood" stories was told in the collection of the clay tablets named The Story of Gilgamesh, where the main character Gilgamesh is on a journey to discover the secret of the eternal life. After his friend Enkidu dies, Gilgamesh started to search for his ancestor Utnapishtim—who apparently has been given the eternal life. When he had found him, Utnapishtim told the Gilgamesh that he had survived the great flood. Utnapishtim continued to say, that God Ea told him to build the big ark, and to take his family on board—together with all the animals in the field. After the storm have lasted for six days occupants of the ark had been fine, and when storm stopped Utnapishtim then released a dove, swallow, and a raven in that order. After the raven did not return, Utnapishtim had realized that there must be dry land nearby. Soon-after the ark lodged on the mountain, and he had released all of the ark occupants from the ark to land—to replenish it. For that act of heroism he was rewarded with eternal life. He also had advised the Gilgamesh to stop looking for the eternal life, but told him about a plant, which can make him stay young. After a long time Gilgamesh had found the plant—but a snake was able to steal it from him. This marvelous Mesopotamian story then continues to tell us that Gilgamesh thereafter went back to his home in the city of Uruk, and had completely abandoned the hope of either immortality, or forever youth. Eventually he had learned that the life you are looking for—you will never find. Epic story!

45.

Leaving things written on the clay tablets was very important for the Mesopotamians. With that technique, they were also able to preserve many other things—like remedies, and the food recipes they left behind. Same as with the epic stories, those remedies, and the recipes, were probably known in oral form for many generations. For example, there is a tablet found that has a recipe for how to prepare goat stew. It says "to mix pieces of goat meat with garlic, onions, and sour milk." Already at that time, they knew they had to protect important tablets—so, for those important tablets they had used better clay— they also had coated it with an extra layer of the clay. Styluses, that have extra sharp triangular tips were invented in the same time, so they would leave nice, sharp marks, into the moist clay—before the tablet would be baked.

46.

In my opinion, one of most interesting tablets was found in 1901. The Babylonian king named Hammurabi, had ruled from 1792 BC to 1750 BC, and had left the Code of Hammurabi written in the clay. That is a famous Babylonian law code of ancient Mesopotamia. The Code has 282 laws explained. They range from the different punishments for the wrong-doings, to the wages of the workers. There are some very detailed laws, like the liability of the house builder, etc. A list of the laws written there is now considered to be kind of very harsh, but keep in the mind that it has been written over 3750 years ago. It was already ancient even when Jesus Christ was born. Here are a few different laws mentioned: Law # 22: "If anyone is committing a robbery and is caught, then he shall be put to death," Law # 104: "If a merchant gives an agent corn, wool, oil, or any other goods to transport, the agent shall give a receipt for the amount, and compensate the merchant therefor. Then he shall obtain a receipt from the merchant for the money that he gives the merchant," Law # 195: "If a son strike his father, his hands shall be hewn off," and most famous, including "an eye for an eye" are Laws from # 196 to # 199: "If a man destroy the eye of another man, his eye shall be put out. If one break a man's bone, they shall break his bone. If one put out the eye of a freeman or break the bone of a freeman he shall pay one gold mina. If one put out the eye of a man's slave or break a bone of a man's slave, he shall pay one-half his value." Outstanding!

47.

Along with the Mesopotamia and the Ancient Egypt, one of the three early civilization was—the Indus Valley Civilization. It goes sometimes under the name Indus-Sarasvati Civilization, because it was thriving along the Indus River, and now the dried Sarasvati River, between circa 3300 BCE to 1300 BCE. A third common name is the Harappa Civilization, named after the Harappa site—which was the first site of this civilization excavated in the 1920s. That advance civilization covered areas of present day Pakistan, northwest India, and northeast Afghanistan. It is possible, that at its peak, it had five million inhabitants. The way they have developed their system of drainage against floods, and the sewerage system, is very contemporary in nature—which is still used in some places at the present. Their houses had inner courtyards, and rooms that resemble bathrooms—it looked like they had covered drains. Houses were built from the baked bricks, and most of the houses had a water supply system. Whole cities were recognized as very urban planning in nature—with many large nonliving buildings in the cities. Inhabitants were marvelous in handicraft—like some terracotta toys I had seen in one picture—they looked like they could be sold in stores today. Let me remind you, I am writing about the civilization which ended over 3000 years ago. Another thing they were great at is metallurgy—as it is obvious they had used copper, lead, and bronze. It's too bad that we don't know much more about this civilization. We can only guess about what had happened with that great civilization to go extinct—a drought, an earthquake, or an epidemic sounds like the best guess, thus far.

48.

Even though, the Indus Valley civilization was very advanced in their planning, and building of the cities—their writing is not understood much. Many unearthed stone, and clay tablets, do have some engraved markings—but it is not really agreed if that represents their writing system. It is surprising, that after being such good craftsmen, that they did not leave any longer scripts—except those symbols carved or painted on the tablets, pottery, terracotta, bronze, etc. Those symbols surprisingly do not show any significant changes, in the long time span. Writings at Mesopotamia were much more developed, and luckily for us, we have found all these interesting stories from the Mesopotamian civilization. Sometimes I think, maybe something is wrong with us—maybe we just don't understand.

49.

The first writing in the Indian subcontinent actually appears in the form of Brahmi script, and it was found on pieces of pottery, dated to the early fourth century BCE, and 33 stone inscriptions on the Pillars of Ashoka—known as Edicts of Ashoka—dated to mid third century BCE. When people think of Ancient India's language—the Sanskrit language usually comes first to mind. Sanskrit is one of the oldest members of Indo-European languages, which dates back to the early second millennium BCE—but none of the Sanskrit scripts that old have been found. It is estimated, that there are over 400 Indo-European languages—in the world. Sanskrit comes from the same group of languages—as most of European languages—including English. The literal meaning of Sanskrit is, refined speech. The most known form of Sanskrit is the Vedic Sanskrit, and Vedas are the oldest Sanskrit literature scripts. They are sacred texts of the religion—Hinduism.

50.

Two major Sanskrit epic books are: The Mahabharata, and Ramayana. Mahabharata is considered the longest epic poem of all times—in total it has 1.8 million words. The name itself could be translated as, Bharata Dynasty, or King Bharata—and is a narrative of the Kurukshetra War. That war was between King Kaurava, and his cousins—Pandava princes. The story is traditionally ascribed to the Vyasa, who is Avatar of the Hindu God—Vishnu. Vyasa is the major character in the story. In this epic script—it states that Ganesh is the one who wrote it down to Vyasa dictation. Ganesh is probably the most worshiped deities, in the Hindu religion. His elephant head makes him easy to be identified. He is considered as remover of obstacles, and Hindu God of intellect, and wisdom. A very popular part of Mahabharata epic is Bhagavad Gita, which is the narrative framework of dialogue between—Pandava's prince Arjuna—and his guide, and charioteer—Hindu God Krishna. The story is exposed to the world through the Sanjay, who is an advisor and charioteer, to the King of Hastinapur, Dhritarashtra—who was involved in the part of the War of Kurukshetra. Great Mahatma Gandhi referred to this part of the epic—as his "spiritual dictionary." Krishna helped Pandava brothers, and on the end of the epic Krishna dies—and Pandava brothers go to Heaven. Traditionally, it marks the beginning of the Hindu age of Kali Yuga, which is the fourth, and the final age of mankind, in their opinion. The Mahabharata contains devotional, and philosophical material.

51.

The Ramayana is another epic work of Hindu literature. It could be translated as—Rama's Journey. It contains 24,000 verses, in seven books. The story follows Rama, who is an avatar of Hindu Supreme God—Vishnu. Rama's wife Sita was abducted by Ravana, the king of Lanka (Sri Lanka). Obviously, Rama was very upset, and had many sleepless nights. His wife Sita, was pregnant with twins, and later gave birth to two boys—Lava, and Kusha. Rama, even knowing that Sita was innocent, had to release her—to keep his pride. The story is loaded with morality, right-actions, and the virtue. As the story goes, Rama was able to kill King Ravana, and he had crowned Vibheeshana—as the king of Lanka. After that, he returned to Ayodhya, and ruled the kingdom. Many people in India believe that it is a true story, and that during his reign was the most beautiful era in history of the India. In his kingdom—lying, cheating, theft, killing, or anything bad did not exist. The Ramayana explores human values, and the concept of Dharma, which teaches us on the end—to do all good.

52.

It is believed, that Vedas are existing for over three thousand years, in oral tradition form—but they were written down in Sanskrit, much later. Veda literally means knowledge. There are four Vedas, and they are: Rigveda, Yajurveda, Samaveda, and Atharvaveda—and all four are classified into the four text types: Samhitas, Aranyakas, Brahmanas and Upanishads. Upanishads is a text that interests me the most—out of all four. That part of Veda's discuss meditation, philosophy, and the spiritual knowledge. The Sanskrit word Upanisad, literally means sitting at the own feet—and that probably refers to sitting down calmly, with feet under you—and listening to the teacher. In Hindu philosophy there are six systems: Yoga, Vedanta, Nyaya, Samkhya,

Vaisheshika, and Mimamsa. The one that catches my attention the most is Vedanta, because it represents knowledge centered understanding. It is focused on self-discipline, self-knowledge, and the meditation. Vedanta is based on the Upanishads—and it is emphasized on spirituality, more than ritualism. Ancient India also have philosophies—that share the concept—but reject Vedas. Those philosophies are called—Nastika. The most popular Indian Nastika philosophies include: Jainism, and Buddhism.

53.

In the form of philosophical language, Sanskrit is used in Jainism, and Buddhism. Here I have to mention one teacher, that I admire a lot—Siddhartha Gautama. He is known by a more common name— Buddha. Historians generally agree, that he had existed as an actual person. His birth place is referred on earlier mentioned engravings in the stone by Emperors Edict of Ashoka. There it says that the Emperor visited Buddha's birth place, which is called Lumbini. That place is in present-day Nepal; it is believed that he lived in the fifth, and the sixth century BCE—lately years from 583 BCE to 400 BCE are considered. In classical philosophy he is a Sage—and that is someone who has attained the wisdom—the wisdom that philosopher seeks. Buddha literally means—awakened one. Even though he was born as a Prince, and had everything he could want—Siddhartha realized material wealth is not the meaning of life. On his four trips outside the palace he noticed four different things—in the real life there was, sick, old aged, dead, and on the last trip he noticed wondering Monk, who had given up everything he owned, to try to find the way to quit suffering in the world. The young prince then said: "I shall be like him." At age 29, it is believed, he had left his palace, and started his journey to discover happiness in the world—and end of his suffering. He tried by different means to obtain the knowledge. First, he mastered two different teachings of Yoga meditation, but was still looking for more. After that he tried another way to find the enlightenment—by starving himself—and that almost had killed him—when he collapsed in the river. He was saved by a village girl Sujata, who gave him some food. Then came the famous story, of him sitting under Bodhi tree—wisdom tree—which is a sort of a fig tree. The tree is named after a place Bodhi, which is located in present-day India. That is where Siddhartha decided never to arise—until he finds the truth. His companions had left him, thinking he had become undisciplined. For 49 days Siddhartha was meditating, and finally, he had found what he was looking for. He announced than, that he had attained Enlightenment—at 35 years old.

54.

That profound peace of mind, that he had found, is called—Nirvana. Since that time, he was called Buddha—by his followers. While meditating Buddha had discovered three great truths, and four Noble truths. In the very simple words—explained by Instilling Goodness School—three great truths are First: Nothing is lost in the universe, for example matter turns into energy, and energy turns into matter—or we are born to our parents, and our children are born to us. Second: Everything changes. It states that life is like a river—ever changing. Sometimes it flows slowly, and smoothly, then it suddenly snags on the curves and rocks out of nowhere—like in the life when we think it's all smooth—then something unexpected happens. And Third: Law of Cause and Effect—this law is known as Karma. Nothing happens to us unless we deserve it. Our thoughts, and the actions determine the kind of life we have. If we do all right things we don't need to fear Karma. His final conclusion was that all the pain is caused by suffering, and that there are steps to eliminate it—that is what Buddhists call the Four Noble Truths. They are as follows: First, There is Suffering, and suffering is common to all. For example, absolutely everyone suffers from something, like birth, sickness, old age, or death—also common to all is that we suffer—because we don't always get what we want, or occasionally we miss somebody that we like. Second: Cause of Suffering. The Buddha explained that people suffer because the ignorance, and the greed. They pay the price for being greedy, and wanting the wrong kind of pleasures. Third: End of Suffering. To stop suffering—you have to stop doing what causes it. The one has to cut off greed, and ignorance, by living the natural and peaceful way. And Fourth: Path to end Suffering. That includes, right view, thought, speech, conduct, livelihood, effort, mindfulness, and concentration. Buddha never spoke harshly to anybody, even if they have opposed him. After he had found what he was looking for—he had spent the rest of his long life preaching about it—and giving the sermons. It was recorded, that he said: "There have been many Buddhas before me, and will be many Buddhas in the future." I love him!

55.

In Egypt they started using hieroglyphs—as characters—for the writing. Simplified glyph Hieroglyphic writing was composed of approximately 500 symbols. For Egyptians, five thousand years ago burial of the dead had significant importance. The use of hieroglyphs was found on many stone monuments, and in the tombs. It was common to engrave, or write hieroglyphs on the wood, stone, or the papyrus. Two popular scripts were developed, one was Hieratic that was mostly used among priests, and Demotic for the popular use.

56.

The essential key moment for modern understanding of Ancient Egyptian literature was the discovery of the black basalt slab stone plate. It is the now famous—Rosetta Stone. It has three script inscriptions in two languages. The first script was Ancient Egyptian hieroglyphics, the second Egyptian demotic script, and the third Ancient Greek. That discovery happened in 1799, by a French soldier near the town of Rosetta—in Egypt. In took some time before Jean-Francois Champollion deciphered hieroglyphs, in 1822. If you wondered, the text contains the list of things Egyptian Pharaoh has done—that are good—for the priest. It is assumed that priests wrote that, to honor the Pharaoh.

57.

For us, at the present day, it is more common to connect ancient Egyptian scripts to papyrus scrolls—then to wood, or stone carvings. That actually might be just in my case, because that is how I remember seeing it—while attending school. I was very impressed by the look of papyrus, and when I went to visit Egypt—as a teenager—one of the things that had impressed me the most, was visiting the papyrus factory. We watched the whole process of making papyrus. It is made from the stem of the plant—Cyperus papyrus. The sticky fibrous inner part of the plant is cut into long strips—which are then placed side by side—on a hard surface, with their edges overlapping. Another layer of the strips is put on the top at a right angle, before being soaked in water. While wet, strips would start fusing together—forming the sheet. After that it is dried under pressure, and finally polished with a round object, which is usually made of the hard wood. To make a long scroll roll, a wooden stick can be attached to the last sheet in the roll, same thing as paper, it would be glued together, to make very long rolls.

58.

Ancient Egyptians were very religious. When in modern times people started discovering many tombs thousands of years old, they notice the same hieroglyph texts present—especially if the tomb belonged to somebody of a higher social status. Those text and images were found engraved into tomb's walls, or on papyrus rolls inside the tomb. It turned out, that it is actually the Ancient Egyptians most important book—and today we call it: Book of the Dead. It has priceless importance for us—to understand its meaning—a few thousand years later. The images, and texts of the Book of the Dead were religious, and magical. It consists of a number of magic spells, which are intended to assist the dead person's journey through the underworld. It was supposed to help the deceased—to control the world around him, or her. As of now, about 192 spells are collected, but they were not put in one continuous book—which means that there are many books found—but none have all of the spells together. During the 25th Pharaonic dynasty book was updated, revised, and standardized—spells were given order, and numbers. There are a few that always catch my attention—one of them is spell 125, where deceased's heart is symbolically weighted, according to their behavior while alive, and spell 30b where the dead person is being judged by God, followed by the list of 42 sins. The Gods looked at the actions of that person, when that person was alive. Those, and a few other spells—in the Book of the Dead, discuss of moral, and ethical standards, which I consider—as another key in life.

59.

Except Book of the Dead, there are many more collections of religious writings—from Ancient Egypt—in the existence now. I will mention a few more, like: Pyramid Text, Coffin Text, Book of Gates, etc. Pyramid Text is considered to be the oldest religious writing in the world. It was found carved on the walls, and sarcophagus of the pyramids—during the Old Kingdom. Pyramid Texts, unlike Coffin Texts, and Book of the Dead, were not illustrated—and were reserved just for the Pharaoh. It is also interesting, that the civilization of Ancient Egypt lasted for over 3000 years, which is longer in time then our whole present history—that we count from the birth of Jesus Christ, a little over 2000 years.

60.

On the same trip to Egypt, with my family—I remember going into pyramids. As a fifteen year old—that was a wonderful experience for me. We went on an eight day vacation to Cairo, and a couple of other cities in Egypt. One of the most important site visits, for me—was the Giza archaeological site. That complex included the massive Great Sphinx, and the three pyramids. We were allowed to go inside one pyramid. There was a small door opening, and a shallow tunnel leading into an underground chamber. The tunnel going into the pyramid is so shallow, that I had hit my head—a few times actually. After going for about 300 feet, we had reached a burial chamber, where finally we were able to stand up. That room was empty of course, because some treasures were transported a long time before—to the British Museum, Berlin's Egyptian Museum, and Italy's Turin Museum. When originally built, over four thousand years ago—the purpose of these Giza pyramids—as well as other pyramids, is believed to be just grave site for deceased Pharaohs, as well as, many things they might have needed in the afterlife—were buried too, with them. As mentioned, in the Book of the Dead— for Ancient Egyptian religion—that things in the afterlife were very necessary. It was believed, that death was just the beginning of the long afterlife journey. There are many pyramids in the world, but only this Giza Great Pyramid was included into the Seven Wonders of the Ancient world, and for at least 3800 years, it was the highest man made structure—anywhere in the world. Just imagine, some of the structures being built today in 2015—to still be the tallest—in the year 5815. Just plain amazing!

61.

During this Bronze Age, that lasted approximately two thousand years—depending again—from region to region, the world had seen a lot of development. Not just for the introduction of written scriptures, but for all areas of life development. Using bronze helped humans in the many fields. Construction of new settlements was contributed to economic growth. Large farms developed, and the search for fertile land—forced large groups of people to move—for the better. A lot of large structures like—towers, and pyramids, were built—some have survived to this day. Many people living at those times, left a legacy—all the way to today. In the Mesopotamia, and Egypt, the Bronze Age started turning into the Iron Age, around 1200 BCE—but for the European, and Chinese, it was around 600 BCE.

62.

Talking about China, their history started there around 1200 BCE, when it is believed, the oldest written records originate. Similar as the Mesopotamian area, their culture was based around two rivers—the Yellow river, and the Yangtze River. Chinese civilization is also, one of the oldest in the world. As mentioned earlier—Chinese for writing use logographs—and easiest confirmed evidence of Chinese writing was found carved on the Oracle bones. The symbols were carved on the pieces of different bones, and on the shells of the turtle. Commonly they were called—dragon bones, and were used for medical purposes, and as they believed—for the communication with royal ancestral spirits. Oracle bones are one of the most important, historical written records, containing information like—complete royal genealogy. Except on the bones, those early Chinese writers used bamboo, and silk, for writing too. Over the years Chinese characters, which are ideograms, and pictographs—have evolved, like everything else. Pictorial drawings were used as phonetic meaning.

63.

I am very impressed with early Chinese literature. Just to get the idea how systematic through Chinese are—I will mention, that they kept consistent, and accurate court records—since the year 841 BCE. Most of their literature is philosophical, and didactic. Confucius (Kong Zi - Master Kong) is of my dearest philosophers—that has ever lived on the Earth. Except being a philosopher, he was a great politician too—and an even better teacher. His works are of key importance— not just for the Chinese culture, and history—but for the whole humankind. Even before the great Confucius, China already had Five Classics, books which are still 3000 years later—very good reads. I will just mention the book names here—and I hope you will do further research. The Five Classics, with common English language translations are: I Ching (Book of Changes), Shih Ching (Book of Songs), Shu Ching (Book of History), Li Ching (Book of Rites), and Ch'un-ch'iu Shih-tai (Spring and Autumn Annals).

64.

Except the Five Classics, early Chinese literature includes the Four Books—which directly involve Confucius. They are: Analects of Confucius, Mencius, Doctrine of the Mean, and Great Learning. It is considered, that Five Classics, and Four Books, collectively create the foundation of Confucianism—which is a philosophical, and the ethical system—also described as a religion. Confucius's doctrine had a basis in Chinese belief, and tradition. What I like about him the most, is that he was preaching of strong family, loyalty, morality, respect of elders, respect between husbands and wives, and maxim "Do not do to others what you do not want done to yourself," mentioned in Analects of Confucius. The whole philosophy of Confucius was for justice, personal and governmental morality, correctness of social relationships, etc. Confucianism became the official state ideology— of the Chinese Han Dynasty, and has probably influenced many other Chinese emperors, and the governments—since then. When I am talking to my kids, almost every day, I am quoting Confucius. Here are a few examples: "Respect yourself and others will respect you," "It does not matter how slowly you go as long as you do not stop," "Life is really simple, but we insist on making it complicated," and "The man who asks a question is a fool for a minute, the man who does not ask is a fool for a life," etc.

65.

As a matter of fact, China between the second and sixth century BC, had so many great authors—that left so many masterpiece writings— whole time is called "Hundred Schools of Thought" for that reason. In between many great authors, I will mention another two: Laozi (Lao Tzu or Zi - Old Master), and Zhuangzi (Chuang Zi - Master Zhuang). In their case I will start with the quotes. First for Laozi: "The journey of a thousand miles begins with a single step," "Those who know do not speak and those who speak do not know," "The truth is not always beautiful, nor beautiful words are always the truth," and "Care about what other people think of you and you will always be their prisoner," and Zhuangzi's: "A path is made by walking on it," or this one: "Rewards and punishment is the lowest form of education," and "To a mind that is still, the entire universe surrenders," etc.

66.

Laozi's book—Tao Te Ching, and Zhuangzi's book named after him—Zhuangzi, are two foundational texts of ethical, and religious tradition—Taoism. Origin of Taoism emphasized living in the harmony with the nature—where Tao means "way," "path," or "principle." Followers of the Taoism even consider Laozi to be deity, in the religious Taoism. Laozi would usually explain his ideas—by the way of paradox, or more precisely—as an analogy. His "way" is all about meditation, senses, and renounce.

67.

About ten years ago, I walked into a big chain book store—as I do sometimes—just to see if any book would catch my attention. There was this smaller in size book, with an eye catching name—Art of War. I thought I'd heard about it before, but I was not sure. Good thing I ended up buying it. So, the book that was written probably about 2500 years ago—still catches the attention of the eye—and it is being sold on bookstores shelves, like any other book just written—that is simply amazing to me. Definitely, that's another Chinese pre-common era time book—that has fascinated me. The Art of War was written by Sun Tzu (Sun Zi - Master Sun), who was a military person (possibly General), tactician, and the strategist. I am sure even now, the same as it used to be for centuries, it has an influence on Western, and Eastern military strategy, tactics, and thinking. Sun Tzu emphasized the importance of positioning during war—and it is known now, that some of the most famous Generals in different wars, used information from this book. Here I will mention a few of the quotes from inside the book: "Appear weak when you are strong, and strong when you are weak," "Know yourself and you will win all battles," "Even the finest sword plunged into salt water will eventually rust," "He will win who knows when to fight and when not to fight," and "Treat your soldiers as your own beloved sons, and they will follow you into the deepest valley." For the end I left the motivational speakers favorite: "You have to believe in yourself," and that was also coined by Sun Tzu, 2500 years ago.

68.

The story about Ancient China I will finish with the—Terracotta Army. It is the fascinating tomb of the Qin Shi Huang—the first Emperor of China. Discovered only in 1974, his tomb is such an amazing funerary art. It is hidden into mound, and its size is extraordinary. It is estimated, that all the pits cover almost 22 square miles. It is believed, that the underground tomb represents the real life size—of the capital Xianyang. What is for sure—the real life size of estimated 8000 warriors, and hundreds of horses—made of terracotta (clay based ceramics). Those terracotta sculptures have many bronze items too—from swords, axes, bows, arrow heads, etc. Horses even have halters. It is believed, that this amazing site's purpose was to protect the emperor, in his afterlife. Because heads, torsos, arms, and legs were created separately—and then assembled—it is counted as one of the first, if not first, assembly line productions. Each workshop even inscribed its name, on the items, to ensure quality control. I was glad to learn, that this site is under protection of the UNESCO.

69.

The first human presence in Mesoamerica is connected to the Paleolithic-Indian period, which lasted from 10,000 BCE to 3500 BCE. It is also believed, that the first settlements had been formed— at that time. There was also the possibility for the establishment of agriculture—during that era. Archaic Era, has a little more evidence;

it lasted from circa 3500 BCE to 2000 BCE, which shows us, that people started living in the permanent villages then. Stone grinding, and pottery, were established at that time too. The Formative Period, which also has a name Pre-classic Era, lasted from 1800 BCE to 200 CE. At that time writing was introduced, also cities and states were formed. Mesoamerican civilization had really established itself during this Era; with the building of pyramids, human sacrifice, the use of corn, complex calendar, etc. Across Mesoamerica a few civilizations developed and flourished, such as: Zapotec civilization, Olmec civilization, Teotihuacan city-state civilization, and the Maya civilization.

70.

In Mesoamerica, history did not start till approximately 600 BCE; and as of now, the earliest writing in that part of the world is the stone with Zapotec inscription. It has the image, of what appears to be dead, or wounded person—and two hieroglyphs written in between the legs. It is accepted to be called hieroglyphs due to the shapes of the glyphs, which are similar to Egyptian hieroglyphs—even though it is believed, that it was developed totally independently. Those symbols are also a combination of logographic, and syllabic values. The earliest Maya script date back between 300 BCE to 200 BCE—and one of the sites with the earliest Maya art has been found at the caves of Naj Tunich. Those caves are very rich with Mayan archeology; that archeological site contains many paintings, a few hieroglyphic texts, and some handprints. According to those findings we can get the picture of their social, and religious life. It is estimated, that this cave was used till about the year 700. Interestingly, Mayan texts consist approximately 700 different glyphs—and about 75% have been deciphered thus far.

71.

The nature of Târtâria tablets is a subject of debate. In 1961, those tablets were found on a Neolithic site in Târtâria, Romania. Possibly, those three tablets found in Europe could be the oldest writing in the world. It is dated to around 5300 BCE, and have symbols that have not been deciphered yet, as of now. Their name is Vinča symbols; and it is connected to the name of the village of the other archeological site—Neolithic site at Vinča, Serbia. That is where the same symbols were discovered—and those symbols may be best described as photo-writing. Some of the Vinča symbols, are also found on the pots, all across the Balkan area in Europe. For some archeologists this could be the oldest writing in the world, but for some others Jiahu symbols, found in the Jiahu site—near Henan, China are even older. Jiahu site is where sixteen distinct markings, on artifacts, had been found—in 1999. This specific Neolithic site dates back to 6600 BCE. The meaning of these symbols, as well as Vinča symbols, is unknown, and again—the best way to describe both is as proto-writing.

72.

There have been some very interesting hieroglyphs found in the island of Crete. Those Cretan hieroglyphs are estimated to be written between 1625 BCE to 1500 BCE. There are number of glyphs representing logograms, and syllabic signs. As they are undeciphered yet—we really know little about them. Another possible writing system used in Ancient Greece is Linear A; it has been found on palaces, and religious writings of Minoan civilization—mostly on Crete, but also in Greece, Turkey, and Israel as well. Same as Cretan hieroglyphs, Linear A signs have not been deciphered yet, so we know very little about that system too. It is estimated that Linear A was created between 2500 BCE to 1450 BCE. Linear B, descended from Linear A, between 1450 BCE to 1200 BCE—and in the 1950s it has been deciphered, in the most part. It is a syllabic script, and was used for writing in the Mycenaean Greek—which is the earliest Greek language. Linear B predates the Greek alphabet by several centuries, and contains around 87 syllabic signs, and around 100 ideographic signs. Mostly, it was found at palace archives at Knossos, Thebes, and Mycenae—but sadly with the fall of the Mycenaean civilization, it was never used again.

73.

Mycenaean Greece was representing the first advanced civilization—in Ancient Greece. Some of their bigger centers of power were: Pylos, Thebes, Athens, and Mycenae—to which this culture owns the name. Mycenae is now an archeological site, about 55 miles southwest of present day Athens. There were also many other settlements in the area under the Mycenaean culture influence. The Mycenaean period became the historical setting for the story of Troy, and much of ancient Greek literature, and mythology. It is widely believed, that the Greek poet Homer was the author of epic stories—Iliad and Odyssey—which was most likely written in the 8th century BCE. According to Homer stories, historians now think that the Trojan War happened between the 13th and 12th centuries BCE. In Iliad, this great Greek poet covered just the last year of war—but from multiple resources, like classical authors such as: Aristophanes, Cicero, Euripides, and especially in the story Aeneid, by the Latin poet Virgil—the whole story was put together—as we know it today.

74.

The Trojan War was between Achaeans (Greeks) and the city of Troy, because Paris of Troy had kidnapped Queen Helen of Sparta—who was the wife of King Menelaus of Sparta. According to the Greek myth, Aphrodite was the goddess of love, beauty, pleasure, and procreation—and she made Helen the most beautiful women in the world. Troy's stealing of pretty Helen was an insult to Agamemnon, the king of Mycenae—because Hellen was his brother's wife. Agamemnon helped his brother when he led an organized expedition of all Greek (Achaean) troops, gathered from every part of Greece, including his own Mycenae, Athens, Crete, Ithaca, Rhodes and Sparta against the City of Troy. They besieged the city for ten years. The city of Troy also had a long list of allies like the Dardanes, Pelasgians and Thracians. Both sides lost many men, and heroes—like Achilles and Ajax on the Achaean side, also Hector and Paris on the Trojan side. On the end, as the myth has it, Achaeans designed a large horse made of wood—and tricked the Trojans. They pretended, like they were sailing off the coast, with their ships. The horse was a symbol of the Trojans, thus they were thinking it was a present from the Greeks. A big mistake was bringing that horse inside the Troy walls. The horse was indeed filled with Achaean warriors—led by Odyssey. Achaeans killed most of the Trojans, except very few, who they imprisoned. After all, Queen Helen was reunited with the Spartan King Menelaus. Luckily for the Romans, Aeneas the leader of the Trojans' Dardanes allies, also third cousin and principal lieutenant of Hector, son of the Trojan king Pram—escaped. He had formed a new tribe. According to the Roman poet Vigil, and based on Roman Mythology, he became an ancestor to Romulus and Remus—as well as, all of the Romans.

75.

According to Homer, in his next book Odyssey, it took the Greek hero Odyssey ten years to return home—to Ithaca. So, ten years of war, and ten years of travels, apparently took the toll; and made him look different. Twenty years later when he came back home, his loyal wife was still waiting for him—but there were many suitors. The story continues, like it came straight out from Hollywood, that Penelope decided finally to get a new husband—but gave them a game to play. She demanded from suitors for her hand to compete in an archery, using Odyssey's bow. Well nobody, even Penelope, had recognized Odyssey—so, he took part of the competition himself. Story has it, that he of course won the competition; there-after he used the arrows to kill all of the suitors. He finally told Penelope who he was—but she did not believe him. Odyssey used the code to convince her, asking her if she remembered that their first bed was made of an olive tree still rooted to the ground. She was all his—again. Another epic story. Historians have found many parallels in the story of Odyssey, and Gilgamesh—especially the story of their journeys to the ends of the Earth. Let me remind you again, both Iliad and Odyssey were written over 2800 years from now; and around 800 years before the estimated birth of Jesus.

76.

After the fall of the Mycenaean civilization, for a few hundred years, little is known about what was happening—because there are no written records. The Mycenaean script was forgotten, and their literacy had been lost. Around 8th to 9th century BCE, Greece was divided into many small self-governing communities—and the first written records began to appear. This time Greeks adopted Phoenician alphabet—and had modified it to create the Greek alphabet. The Phoenician alphabet was originally derived from Egyptian hieroglyphs. Because Phoenician merchants traveled across the Mediterranean world, and their alphabet was easy to use—many cultures also have adopted it, and modified it. Not only the Greek alphabet—but also Latin, Arabic, Hebrew, and a few more alphabets descended from the Phoenician alphabet. Some of the oral traditions of lore started to be written in Greek at that time, like the Trojan War story, mentioned above, that happened around 12th or 13th century BCE—and was written down, approximately between 8th and 9th century BCE.

77.

The Classical period of Ancient Greece was particularly interesting, in my opinion. It flourished during 5th and 4th century BCE. Foundation for modern civilization was created with it. Scientific thought, artistic thought, western politics, literature, theater—and best of all for me—philosophy, bloomed during this period. A few of my heroes lived during this time period; I'll start with Herodotus, Socrates, Plato, Aristotle, and Alexander the Great. In 540 BCE, Persia conquered the City of Ionia—who left native tyrants to rule. These natives were nominated by Persians satraps. Between 499 BCE and 493 BCE, the revolt by Ionians was crushed by the Persian King—Darius the Great. That victory made him realize that Persians should conquer all of the Greek cities. The Persian invasion on Greece started in 492 BCE. Relatively quickly, they established control of a few cities—including Thrace and Macedon. When they tried to attack Athens, the famous Battle of Marathon happened. Lore has it, that after Persian forces had been beaten by Pheidippides, a Greek soldier, or messenger, ran 26.2 miles without stopping, all the way to Athens—to announce victory. Hence, the modern day race called Marathon—is set for 26.2 miles. That battle drew Persians from Greece for ten years. In 480 BCE Xerxes I of Persia, son of King Darius, started a new invasion on Greece—and captured some Greek areas again. After Persians lost at the Battle of Salamis, and the Battle of Plataea—that had ended the Persian invasion. There were a few more Persian attacks on Greece before 549 BCE, but it is believed, it had stopped with a peace treaty. That treaty, which brought peace, was negotiated by Callias, an Athenian politician; and this document is called Peace of Callias—in history books.

78.

Those-days Greek cities were becoming stronger, and more developed, and the need for education on philosophy, art, science and theatre—had a high demand. Education was mostly private, in most cities in Ancient Greece. After the Classical Period, some city-states established Public schools. Those days, kids did not study to get a good job, they studied to become effective citizens. Usually, wealthy families were sending their boys to learn how to read, write, or play musical instruments. Boys were also trained as athletes—which by gaining the body strength, they could have possibly used in the case of military service. Some girls also learned how to read and write—but were expected to manage the household. Schooling would end at age 18, and it was followed by military training—for a year or two. Poet Homer was described as the first teacher—and his works were models for writing, and speaking.

79.

Herodotus was a Greek writer and historian that wrote only one book—Historia. It was a special kind of book that explained things that had happened in the past—but also covered many other areas—including geography. That book actually gave a name to history. He lived in the fifth century Greece, and his book is believed to be written—between 450 BCE, and 420 BCE. I definitely think that Herodotus knew the secret to life—when he wrote: "Historia (Inquiry); so that the actions of people will not fade with time." Herodotus mentions Iliad and Odyssey, as works of Homer, and went about hundred years back in explaining the events—that he collected orally from multiple resources—before he wrote them down. He also traveled intensively. Many stories were a combination of his travels, and oral folk-tale motifs. It has been noticed that he collected all his materials systematically, and critically. The main source of information for Greco-Persian wars are found in his book, just as an example. Roman philosopher Cicero, first of all, gave him the title: "Father of History." As mentioned above, his master-piece, also included geographical, and ethnographical information. He was accurate, as much as possible, for the majority of the stories he wrote, although some stories were probably fanciful—and it is noticed that he preferred the element of show and entertainment. In antiquity Herodotus was criticized by historians many times, but what is more important—is that modern historians, and philosophers, have a positive opinion of him. Here is a little of his wisdom: "Of all men's miseries the bitterest is this one: To know so much and to have control over nothing," "If a man insisted on always being serious, and never allowed himself a bit of fun and relaxation, he would go mad or become unstable without knowing it," "Men trust their ears less than their eyes," and "Force has no place where there is need of skill."

80.

Socrates, who was a Greek philosopher, was born in circa 470 BCE. Because he did not write any books himself—there are some doubts, if he in fact, was a real person. All we know about Socrates comes from two of his students, philosopher Plato, and historian Xenophon. For that reason he is a very enigmatic figure. In a series of dialogs written by Plato, and Xenophon, most people notice that they idealize him—which is fine with me. Socrates is credited, as one of the founders of Western philosophy. Through Plato's written dialogues, Socrates is known for his contribution to moral philosophy—called Ethics, that recommending concepts of right, and wrong, and a few other philosophical fields. To solve the problem, Socrates would break the problem into a few questions—and by answering them, a person would found the answer to the whole problem. Today we call that— the scientific method. He is probably the most famous for the concept of Socratic Paradoxes, like the statement translated—as "I know that I know nothing." He also believed that virtue, is the knowledge, and that the best thing for people would be to focus on the pursuit of virtue—like moral excellence, and goodness—rather than the pursuit of anything else. Socrates was quoted saying, that his ideas are not his own, rather of his teachers—like Prodicus, and Anaxagoras—and three women, his mom, priestess Diotima, and Aspasia. In the Plato's monologue of the Apology, it is mentioned that Socrates, was active in the battles of Amphipolis, Delium, and Potidaea—for Athens army, but obviously it was not enough to save him, from the trial that Athens had against him. On the trial against him, Socrates stood before a jury of 500 Athenians, and was accused of "refusing to recognize the gods recognized by the state," and of "corrupting the youth." Unfairly, Socrates was sentenced to death, by hemlock poisoning, in 399 BC. If he recommended exile, it is believed now, the court would have probably agreed. He accepted the judge's final decision and drank the poison, rather than pleading for mercy—and going into exile.

81.

Plato was a Classical Greece philosopher—who was an essential figure of spreading the knowledge. He was born in circa 423 BCE. It is believed, that he was born into a family of higher social status—and for that reason, he probably had very good education—from the best teachers at that time. Most likely he was instructed in philosophy, grammar, theology, music, and gymnastics. Luckily for us, Plato wrote a lot about one of his teachers, which I just mentioned—Socrates. It is believed, that many ideas that he had put under Socrates, were actually Plato's own. He showed big respect, to his teacher. For me, the most important thing that he did, was the establishment of the first institution of higher learning in the western world—he called it Academy. It is estimated, that Plato opened his school of learning, at 385 BCE. Different subjects were taught in Academy, from philosophy to astronomy, biology, political theory, and mathematics. In Plato's dialogues, he teaches a wide range of subjects, from philosophy to logic, religion, mathematics, aesthetics, political theory, biology, and ethics. He formed the Theory of Forms, or ideas where objects are abstract, and do not exist in time and space—for what reason they are non-physical. One of the most famous thoughts in the school of Platonism, is Platonic love, where love is chaste and acceptable by moral standards—based on respect. That is when you love somebody, very much, but without physical contact. His Academy was open until 529 CE, when Roman Emperor Justinian I closed it—because he feared it was a threat to Christianity. Here are just a few quotes taken from his writings: "Ignorance, the root and stem of every evil," "I'm trying to think, don't confuse me with facts," "There are three classes of men; lovers of wisdom, lovers of honor, and lovers of gain," "The heaviest penalty for declining to rule is to be ruled by someone inferior to yourself," and the one, where he showed he knew the secret to life: "Education is teaching our children to desire the right things." There were many students of his, here are just a few—like Heraclides Pontius, Eudoxus of Cnidus, Crantor, Phillip of Opus—and one everyone has heard about—the amazing Aristotle.

82.

Aristotle was born in the Macedonian city of Stagira, on the northern part of Classical Greece, in 384 BC. When he was eighteen, he joined Plato's Academy, in Athens—and was there until he was 37 years old.

He was such a great philosopher, and scientist—that wrote on many subjects—from logic to physics, metaphysics, biology, zoology, poetry, music, rhetoric, and linguistics. It is believed, that he has influenced, even after he died—till today, more scholars, and future big thinkers, and leaders, in more fields—then any other teacher, ever. The list is so long, that a whole book could be written about it. In 343 BCE, he was called by King Philip II of Macedon—to become a tutor—to his son Alexander. As soon as he arrived, he was appointed, as the head of royal academy—of Macedon. Except for the future ruler Alexander the Great, he also gave lessons to two other future kings—Ptolemy, and Cassander. Around 335 BCE, Aristotle had returned to Athens, where he started his own school—Lyceum. It is estimated, that in the following 12 years, he was most productive—and that is when he wrote many of his works. By that time he shifted his views on life, from his teacher's Platonism to empiricism—where he stated that all knowledge comes primarily from sensory experience, ultimately based on perception. For him, memory, is the ability to hold onto perceived experience—and the mind has the ability to distinguish if something is actually happening now—or if it happened in the past. In today's words, he imagined that there is something, except the brain, like what we call today—a hard drive—in the body that we use when it is necessary to pull information, from our experiences. I personally think—it is part of soul. Perception involves signals, in the outer nervous system, to stimulate sense in the body. His specialty was to teach natural philosophy, which today is considered physics, biology, and other natural sciences—and that part was explained—in his books: Physics, Metaphysics, Politics, On the Soul, Poetics, and Nicomachean Ethics. In the book On the Soul, he explains three kinds of souls; the vegetative soul, the sensitive soul, and the rational soul. He suggested that humans have a rational soul. Aristotle proposed, that except for the four known earthly elements—Earth, Water, Air and Fire, which was proposed by Empedocles, that there is a fifth element that he called—Aether, which later was renamed to Ether. It is the best of his ideas, in my opinion. According to him, that is Divine substance, which is made of spheres that exist—but we don't see. Similar to the Chinese philosophers, he also said: "Knowing yourself is the beginning of all wisdom," and "He who has overcome his fears will truly be free." Here a few more quotes of his wisdom: "Hope is a waking dream," "Poverty is the parent of revolution and crime," "Happiness depends upon ourselves," "No great mind has ever existed without a touch of madness," and "Happiness is the meaning and the purpose of life, the whole aim and end of human existence."

83.

As the Phoenician people traveled all around the Mediterranean, as mentioned earlier, they had spread their writings. People all around that area enjoyed listening to epic stories, and marvelous architecture of Mesopotamia. What is most important—they had influenced locals to start writing. As I wrote earlier, Greeks first adopted Phoenician cuneiform syllabic alphabet, to make their own. With knowledge of the early Phoenician alphabet, and mostly based on the Euboean Greek alphabet, Etruscans developed their own—Etruscan alphabet. That was the first alphabet on the Italian peninsula. Historians estimate now that during the late Bronze Age, between 1200 BCE and 900 BCE, Indo-European people migrated to the Italian peninsula; and there are numerous relics of the nomadic steppe culture in Italic people, like for example, specifically shaped iron arrowheads. During the Iron Age many of those people founded their own tribes. Some of the Indo-European tribes were Latins, Falisci, Umbri, Osci, Samnites and Sicels. The Italian peninsula already had pre Indo-European tribes—like Etruscans, Sherden and Camunni, in addition to settlements of other European people like Continental Celtic—and Illyrian people. Also, Greek people living on Italian peninsula at that time—were Dorians, Achaeans, Ionians, and others.

84.

The Etruscan tribe developed the first alphabet of all italic people. That was of course essential, to learn how to write. Their civilization endured for several hundred years, before they were assimilated— into Roman Republic—in the late 4th century BCE. By the mixture of legend, and Roman mythology—the city of Rome was founded— in 753 BCE, by Romulus and Remus—abandoned at birth twins. According to the legend, they survived by feeding on the she-wolf. Sometime after, shepherd Faustulus found them, and he raised them as his own children. As adults the twins went on together, to build the city—but after altercation, Romulus killed Remus, and named the new city—Rome. According to Roman poet Virgil, in his book Aeneid, as I mentioned earlier—he claimed that the ancestor of Romans was the Trojan prince Aeneas—who escaped after the fall of Troy, and after a series of adventures around the Mediterranean Sea— landed on the Italian peninsula—near what would later be Rome. By archeological evidence—people were definitely living in that area— in the eight century BCE, and most likely were mixed Latins, Sabines, and Etruscan. A famous Latin tribe was living about 60 miles away, and it is believed, that people in Rome spoke the Latin language. The Latin tribe stayed separated from the city of Rome, until they were united, in 338 BCE.

85.

Even though Etruscans started their history with learning how to write, not many of their writings have been found. There are some tombstone inscriptions in Etruscan language. We know that they were good artists—with many vases, statues, and jewelry found. Some of the arts have inscriptions, and part of an Etruscan book made of linen—has also been found. Texts can be read, but as of now, the real meaning, has not been figured out yet. It is well known—that many other tribes alphabets, like: Latin, Oscan, and Umbrian, have a foundation in the Etruscan alphabet. As Rome progressed, in all new occupied areas, the Latin language was installed as a dominant language—and the Latin alphabet would eventually become—one of the most widely used alphabets—in the whole world. The oldest inscription, is believed to be found, on "Black Stone"—in the Roman Forum. It is estimated, that it was written around 600 BCE. As Latin remained to be the main written language of the Roman Empire, Greek was the main language spoken by the well-educated elite. That is because most of the literature was written in Greek. When Rome became an Empire, it is estimated that 20% of the world population—was talking in Latin. It is interesting, that in the eastern half of Roman Empire, Greek language always stayed more in use. After that area separated from the Roman Empire, and became the Byzantine Empire, Greek became the official language of the Byzantine government.

86.

Regardless of the Byzantine Empire, the Latin language was still spreading—all across other parts of Europe. Over the years, new dialects of Vulgar Latin were created, which led to a few of the new Romance languages like: Spanish, Portuguese, Romanian, and French. What is good about early Latin writers, is that they started writing on separate pages—each with numbers listed. As mentioned before—old writings were in long scrolls—and it was hard to find a specific part of the script. Latin writers started writing a table of contents, like we still do now-days, so it makes it much easier to find the desired part of the book—especially if you look for that page number. Even though, Latin itself is not widely spoken today, it still survived through professional terminology, especially in the medical industry. And there is still one country in the world where it is the official language—it is Vatican.

87.

The part of the Ancient Roman civilization that I admire the most—is when they created the government system called—Roman Republic—that lasted from 509 BCE, to 27 BCE. Two Consuls led the government, and they were elected annually, by the citizens, and advised by Senate. The Republic was highly developed, and was very systematic. It was based on tradition, and morality. That society was able to obtain great architectural and technological achievement. That system had built large roads, monuments and palaces—some of the legal, and legislative structures are still observed in modern nations, and organizations. The Roman Republic's contribution to law, politics, art, and literature is remarkable.

88.

Many times in this book, as in history in general, we measure the time before the birth of Jesus Christ, as BCE (before common era), rather than the BC (before Christ), even though, it is in the fact connected to the life of Jesus Christ. In Roman times, before sixth century CE, people measured years since the founding of Rome—and in the 6th century—it was more common to count the years since the reign of the Roman emperor Diocletian—who lived circa 245 CE to 311 CE. Around 523 CE a Christian monk named Dionysius Exiguus (in English known as Dennis the Little), was asked by papal chancellor— to prepare calculations of the dates of Easter—in accordance with decrees of the council of Christian bishops, appointed by Constantin the Great—for the 325 CE meeting in Nicaea. Dionysius decided to calculate Easter's date from the time of Jesus' birth, rather than from the time of Emperor Diocletian, since that emperor was a persecutor of Christians. Mr. Dionysius was fluent in Latin, and Greek—and probably used a lot of documents to determine the year of Jesus' birth, but ended up being wrong, most likely. The Gospel of Matthew in the Bible, mentions that Jesus was born under the reign of King Herod the Great, who actually died four years before Dionysius year one. So, either Mr. Matthew was wrong, or Jesus was born before 4 CE. If Matthew was right, then Dionysius' calendar, that almost the whole world follows—is wrong. That's why I think saying before, and after common time, BCE or CE, is the best option. Lately, many historians predict that Jesus was born between 7 BCE, and 4 BCE

89.

Regardless when exactly Jesus was born, he was one of the best teachers the world has ever seen. Most scholars agree, that he existed as a real person, and Christians believe that he is the son of God. It is widely accepted that Jesus lived about two thousand years ago—and that most likely he was a Galilean Jewish rabbi—who was spreading positive thoughts, and giving inspiring preaching sermons. In those days, people used to have just one name, and it was common to connect them to the place from where they come from. According to that, Jesus (Yeshua or Joshua) was known as—Jesus of Nazareth. Jewish historian Josephus, in the late first century, and Roman historian Tacitus in the early second century, have both mentioned Jesus in their writings. With the formation of Christianity, next to Jesus' name—was added Christ—which is the Greek word for Messiah. That title originated with Judaism, which means anointed one, or savior of the people. Jews do not accept Jesus, to be Messiah. Most what we know about his life comes from the books, called Gospels. They are a part of the Christian New Testament Bible, and Gospels were written many years after Jesus died. Of the many gospels written in antiquity about Jesus' life, only four gospels came to be accepted, as part of the Christian New Testament. It is hard to literally believe in everything that was told about him there, but deep inside me, I think that he existed—and that he preached all good things. Personally, I reject the idea to call him—the son of God.

90.

"Ars longa, vita brevis," which is popularly rendered as—Art is long, life is short—is a Latin translation of a quote, by a great ancient Greece physician—Hippocrates. He lived in fourth, and fifth century BCE Greece. In his book Aphorism, the amazing Hippocrates chose to have this written as his opening lines. Originally in Greek, he said it backwards Life is short, art is long, but the world later accepted the Roman Latin translation—as more known. Regardless which way you say it, it still has the same meaning. Even though he was concentrated on the medical field mostly, I would translate it: As you leave art, where art figuratively represents a metaphor for any work of value, it will live forever, even after you die. "Art" could be a painting, any kind of craft, monument, fountain, book, song, etc. If you are a doctor, do good "art" and you'll be remembered. Anything you create gets a life of its own, and later sometimes, it can become even larger than your life, in some cases it becomes an Era. Like in a case of the great artist Alphonse Mucha, in the late nineteenth century CE. Mr. Mucha created very influential pieces of art, and pretty much started a new Era—famously called Art Nouveau. Coming back to Hippocrates; even though he is considered, and called, the "Father of western medicine," and is best known for his discoveries in the medical field—again, I find him to be one of the fathers of discovering the meaning to life, and someone who definitely knew—what was the purpose of his life.

91.

With this last story—I am finishing BCE stories that fascinated me the most, and stories of BCE teachers, that taught me the most. I find written records—as the best sources in search for meaning, even though, through all virtues mentioned above, you can find it too. Most advices, that we all hear from contemporary inspirational writers, were said; and many times written, a long time ago—even centuries before Jesus. It is not always that people intentionally copy what somebody else has said, or wrote, sometime earlier in the past. Sometimes, we people, produce the same conclusions in our own ways. Like song writers, they sometimes come up with very delightful song lines themselves; but many times, the same lines had been thought of by some other songwriter, earlier. I am doing my best to connect quotes to their original authors—which in most cases goes back to Ancient Chinese, Greek, or Roman philosophers, indeed. In the rest of the first part of this book, I will concentrate more just on discovering the secret to the meaning of life, and people that have impressed me.

92.

I know that you have already gotten the idea—what I think the meaning of life is, because I have tried to lead you in that direction. It took me many years, of my own studying, and investigation—to come to this conclusion. Being at work, many times, hundred hours a week, had some benefits for me. In between transfers, when I did not drive people—I have read hundreds of books, especially, before I started bringing the Internet to the car with me, books were my best friend. Do not get me wrong, the Internet is one of the best innovations in the history of human kind, but it also takes away your time, for useless looking at things, we do not need. Except reading, I have spent every day, at least for a couple of hours thinking of—what the meaning to life is. To fulfill our life's meaning, we have to leave the legacy. Legacy is something—that the world, or just our family, will remember us for—when we die. The bigger the influence on the world we leave— the bigger remembrance of us, will be. Still, any good legacy is good, regardless of the impact that it has left on the world. A couple of times, I have heard from people—how happy they were, when they discovered some notes, or letters left to them by their parents, or grandparents. They are holding on to those, as if they are the largest treasures on this world. Let's say: In the case if you leave a great work of art, song, or extraordinary book behind you—not only your family, but the whole world will possibly celebrate you. There are different kinds of legacies you can leave, except material evidence. For example, if you happen to be in the right situation at the right time, and save somebody's life—and become a hero. If that story becomes news, or even if it does not, you will still get a good score for your soul. If a sportsman wins a tournament, or medal, why do you think they are so happy? Deep inside, they know that they have accomplished something big. Sometimes, they don't even realize that they have fulfilled their purpose in life—but they still feel great. That is because their subconscious knows, it knows that they did something great, hence all the emotions erupt. The important thing is, that you have to act accordingly thereafter, by doing all the right things. One act of heroism doesn't buy you a ticket to glory—for your whole life.

93.

There are people that did great things at one point in their life, then did some terrible things in the following years—so, they technically erased all of the good things they did before. On the other hand there are some people, that did some pretty bad things in one part of their life; and after they realized that they were wrong, luckily they started doing good things. It is never too late to start doing good things. Leo Tolstoy is one of my greatest teachers. He was a Count, which is equivalent of Earl in British aristocracy, and one of the greatest novelists—if not the greatest. According to great novelists like: Virginia Wolf, Thomas Mann, and Fyodor Dostoyevsky—Tolstoy, indeed, was the greatest. The books he left behind are among the most respected in the history of writing. It is hard to find an educated person that has not heard of his masterpieces such as: War and Peace or Anna Karenina, in between many of his books. In his own words he wrote, in his book Confection: "I killed men in war and challenged men to duels in order to kill them. I lost at cards, consumed the labor of the peasants, sentenced them to punishments, I lived loosely, and deceived people. Lying, robbery, adultery of all kinds, drunkenness, violence, murder—there was no crime I did not commit, and in the spit of that people praised my conduct and my contemporaries considered and consider me to be a comparatively moral man. So I lived for ten years." After realizing how wrong he was, Mr. Tolstoy had changed completely, gave up smoking, and drinking of alcohol—and even became vegetarian. It was said, that when a big famine had hit Russia hard in 1873, he decided to help peasants, and believe it or not, stopped writing Anna Karenina for a year—so he could organize the aid. He said: "I cannot tear myself away from living creatures to bother about imaginary ones." His family assisted him with his remarkable help, and especially after the 1891 famine, they had spent two years helping people in need—by collecting money, and even working in the soup kitchens. He developed a nonviolent resistance idea, which was very influential on amazing historic peace-activist figures like: Martin Luther King Jr., and Mohandas Karamchand (Mahatma) Gandhi. Gandhi actually had active correspondence with Tolstoy. The view on life in Tolstoy's words is: "The sole meaning of life is to serve humanity," which was later completely utilized—by the good man Mahatma (which is Sanskrit word for a great soul) Gandhi. A whole book could be written just about Tolstoy's quotes, but then again, I do not want to make this book too long—so I will just mention a few: "Everyone thinks of changing the world, but no one thinks of changing himself," "When you love someone, you love the person as they are, and not as you'd like them to be," "Anything is better than lies and deceit," "Wrong does not cease to be wrong because the majority share in it," "God is the same everywhere," and my sister's favorite: "If you want to be happy, be."

94.

I came up to conclusion, that there are three kinds of people—who I consider to belong to different groups. First, and best—are those that have concluded the answer to the meaning of life. They have mentioned it while writing, or publicly speaking—like for example, the earlier mentioned Hippocrates, whose opening lines in his Aphorism book showed, that he knew he was making history. I am sure that he was one hundred percent certain, that it is the most important thing in life to leave a legacy behind. Another example of a man who, in my opinion, knew the meaning to life is Nikola Tesla. Tesla was a great physicist, electrical, and mechanical engineer, futurist, and amazing inventor—who had about 300 patents under his name. He was most known for his discovery of AC electrical systems, but Tesla was also a pioneer in radio, radar, and wireless technology too. While he was alive, his work was not too much appreciated—but regardless, he kept on working, because he knew that he was leaving a huge legacy behind him. When he died many had forgotten him, but since 1990-ties he had regained respect, and now-days it is hard to find a person who has not heard of him. People around him did not listen to his words closely, but he kept on telling them secrets. Here are a few of his quotes: "My brain is only a receiver, in the Universe there is a core from which we obtain knowledge, strength and inspiration, I have not penetrated into the secrets of this core, but I know that it exists," "One must be sane to think clearly, but one can think deeply and be quite insane," "Of all things, I liked books best," "If you want to find the secrets of the universe, think in terms of energy, frequency and vibration," "I don't care that they stole my idea, I care that they don't have any of their own," and the one—which makes me think that he knew the secret—is: "The present is theirs; the future, for which I really worked, is mine." With bigger recognition of his works—his words are finally coming to be true.

95.

The second group includes people, that have accomplished amazing things—and with that pursuit, they have fulfilled the meaning of their life—but they have not realized it. Some of them died many years ago, and I am sure they ended up high—on the afterlife's list. That afterlife, I will explain more in the religion section. And again, there are some living now among us—that have fully fulfilled their life meaning, but have not come up with that conclusion. Again, they know that they did something great, but sometimes those extraordinary people just take it for granted, and can damage, or erase their pursuit. There is a long list of successful people that have damaged their legacy—for reasons mention above. Many times they took things for granted, especially sportsman, and actors. All they needed was to stay good for the rest of their life, but because they did not realize the worthy prize they owned, they eventually repent. Most of them, when they get old, feel sorrow, and will regret it—all because of their lust, or their megalomania.

96.

I will mention some individuals, who belong to my second group of people, who have achieved their life's meaning. I am very impressed with an amazing young girl—Laura Dekker, a sailor. She was born in 1995, and in 2009 she announced her plan to circumnavigate the globe—as the youngest person ever. The Dutch court delayed her trip; but she was still able to pursue that extraordinary task, and at the age of 16 years and 123 days—she completed her mission. Apparently, as a very young girl she received the book, Maiden Voyage, which is a memoir of around the world sailing written by another extraordinary lady—Tania Aebi; and that book made a heavy influence on her. I have watched Miss. Dekker's movie Maidentrip, that she recorded while sailing—and one story she mentioned in the movie—proved to me, that she knows the secret. While visiting French Polynesia she said: "All the islands are different, people are different, even cultures are different...in Europe and Holland they are thinking only about money, money is the most important thing, raising the family, getting the car, getting the house, getting kids and then DIE." That is it! That is how people live in most places, not only Europe, and Holland. They are just running, running to make the money, buy the house, pay the bills—and eventually dying without even realizing they have ever lived. All she needs to do now—is to live a good life. She has achieved her life's purpose; perhaps even not fully realizing it—at a very young age, and will be remembered in the history of humankind.

97.

Another person—that was amazing since his childhood is Tiger Woods. I had considered him as a role model for my generation, same goes for David Beckham, Enrique Iglesias, and Angelina Jolie, which I still admire; maybe for the reason that we were all born in 1975. Due to my job, I happened to meet Tiger Woods, twice. For over five years we were actually living in the same part of town, just about three miles apart—off the same main road. For that reason, I looked into his life even deeper, especially, as it looked like he was doing all the right things in life—he was my hero. He is still the youngest person ever to reach the number one ranking on the professional golf world ranking list, at the age of 21 years and 167 days old, in 1997. That's the day that he pretty much reached his life's purpose. I wish he had realized how important his achievement was. As we all know, he admitted infidelity to his wife, and gave a public apology in February of 2010. In his statement, which I watched on CNN, he said: "The issue involved here was my repeated irresponsible behavior. I was unfaithful. I had affairs. I cheated. What I did is not acceptable... ...but I convinced myself that normal rules didn't apply. I never thought about who I was hurting. Instead, I thought only about myself." Where, with his own words, he thought that regular rules don't apply to him, he showed me that he had no clue of his life's meaning. Life rules apply to everybody— from the minimum wage worker to the billionaire, employed to unemployed, amateur sportsman to professional sportsman—even from toll booth attendant to King or Queen, everybody! His legacy is too large to be totally destroyed, but Mr. Woods definitely made big damage to it. If he had just realized that he have achieved his life's purpose by winning all those tournaments, and having a beautiful family—all he needed was to live a good life. As he publicly admitted, he was Buddhist; only if he had listened to his teacher Buddha, or if he read Dhammapada—which is a collection of the Buddha's sayings, where Buddha apparently said: "All that we are is the result of what we have thought: it is founded on our thoughts and made up of our thoughts. If a man speak or act with an evil thought, suffering follows him as the wheel follows the hoof of the beast that draws the wagon.... If a man speak or act with a good thought, happiness follows him like a shadow that never leaves him," Tiger would have realized, not to behave like he did. In simplified words of what Buddha said; all we think, or do, is recorded, even if nobody knows what we have done, it still exists—and it cannot be deleted. Our doings, and thoughts get a life of their own, as I said. If Tiger only knew. Anyways, I wish him all the best. Now Ricardo Kaká, one of the best footballers ever—lives in that same neighborhood. Kaká has won pretty much everything one soccer player can win in his life—and he has a wonderful family. I started looking at his life very closely, since he moved to Orlando, into that community close to my neighborhood, recently. It looks like Kaká is a perfect role model to all young kids, and I hope he stays like that forever. He has definitely achieved his purpose in life, and all he has to do now—is to stay on the right track—for the rest of his life. Just going to an Orlando City soccer club game, or looking at his internet social network accounts—shows us how big of a respect Kaká has. That is for the reason, that he is a great guy.

98.

The third group of people, are those that have not reached their purpose in life, and they definitely have not unveiled the meaning to life—even if they think they have. If you think deeply, how many people do you know that belong to the third group? The answer might surprise you. I would say over ninety percent. You might think, "There is no way, just look at my boss, he is a millionaire, and he has definitely reached the purpose." Well, sorry but you are most likely wrong. Being rich is not a requirement to find your purpose in life—it can help you, but not necessarily—will buy you the purpose. Money cannot buy it, your personality can earn it. Remember, your doings, and even thoughts—have created a life of their own, and they follow you everywhere. Many of you get to know, and become friends with some people that have done extraordinary things, like some doctors—that have saved many lives, or some famous sportsman, actor, singer etc. Those mentioned, qualify for the first, or second group—depending on their real life behavior. But think again, how many of those people, an average person can call a friend. It looks to me—that those famous people are spending most of their time with alike—like maxim "like attract like" says. The bottom line is, that the average citizen is just dreaming of becoming friends with one of them. With my job I happened to drive some very interesting, and famous people—some of them definitely have reached their purpose, and some despite being incredibly rich have no idea what the meaning of life is. I have listened, not intentionally—but still had to hear it, to so many cell phone conversations, where people admitted to cheating on their spouse, or talking bad about some friends or family. They even asked me to take them to places where they can get what they are looking for—which I never do—explaining that I have no idea where they can find it. It looks to me, as if the more money they had, the easier they were a target to misbehavior.

99.

Many times, I have heard people telling stories—of how they had to fire somebody in their company, but one made me think about it, all day. There was one big company conference in Orlando, and on the way to the airport, this gentleman, that I was driving—was saying, that he had to fire the employee, for stealing. He said—that his company had prepared presents for their employees—which were put in the bags, filled with some electronics. In each room, they left paper notes for their employees—to come to the company's desk downstairs, and pick up their gift. One employee, whose roommate colleague was a no show, came with two notes—and told them that he is picking up both gifts, for him, and his roommate—and received both, indeed. Well, somebody in the company later realized, that the other guy was not present—and it was understood that they had to be present at the meeting, to collect the gift. The gentleman I was driving, had to fire the guy—who collected both gifts, on the spot. He mentioned, that the fired guy had a high income. That all day I was thinking about the fired guy—even though it had nothing to do with me. For a few hundreds of dollars, he had lost a good job, and the worst thing—he is a liar, and a thief—from now on. If he knew the meaning to life, I am sure he would never have done it. I gave this simple example, from my life's school, because it can happen to anybody—it only takes a moment of negligence, to do the wrong thing—and sorrow stays forever, I am sure. Well, I like my job, because—almost every day, I learn, or realize something new. Misbehaved people were my teachers, they thought me not to do bad things—I have learned from their experiences.

100.

Even though I am not agreeing with many things written, and said by the great German philosopher Friedrich Nietzsche, and French philosopher Jean Paul Sartre—I still admire them a lot. In addition, I do not agree with philosophical doctrines of nihilism, and existentialism they supported, respectively—but I still consider them as my teachers. I also do not agree with how they lived their personal life, but in their books they have some brilliant lines about life in general. Sounds like a paradox—but it is true. Here are some quotes, from Nietzsche's books, that I find very educative, and inspirational: "I'm not upset that you lied to me, I'm upset that from now on I can't believe you," "Become who you are," "There is more wisdom in your body than in your deepest philosophy," "I know of no better life purpose than to perish in attempting the great and the impossible," and the one I have spent the most time thinking about, and at one point of my life, I was repeating it to myself as a motto, is: "That which does not kill us makes us stronger." Based on my experience, and of the experience of all people in the world—that quote makes so much sense. Every time we go through some difficult point of life, if we unwillingly get to a similar situation—in life later again, we act much more prepared, and definitely stronger. French philosopher, Jean Paul Sartre, had an extraordinary writing career with numerous great works—but I find his open relationship, with fellow French writer, Simone de Beauvoir, a little bit odd. Regardless of how Sartre, or Nietzsche lived their personal life—many times through the words of their fictional characters in their books, they taught me a lot about life. Some of their statements started whole new philosophical ideas. Here are a few of Sartre's quotes from his books: "If you're lonely when you're alone, you're in bad company," "Man is condemned to be free; because once thrown into the world, he is responsible for everything he does. It is up to you to give a meaning (to life)," "Words are loaded pistols," "All that I know about my life, it seems, I have learned in books," and probably the most quoted one: "We are our choices."

101.

Life is a challenge, from childhood—all the way till we finish our life, we constantly worry about different things. It seems, that there is always something to bother us. There are always some obstacles— we have to fight with. One person does not understand another— because sometimes we think our own obstacles are the worst in the whole world—but for somebody else those are very easy to deal with. One time during 2009, I drove one gentleman to the airport—he called one major airline, on the phone to complain. He told the airline representative—that on the way to Orlando, he was not admitted into First Class club—because his pass was blocked for some reason. He was acting like it was the end of the world, insisting, that he does not want that to happen again. It looked like he was in tears. In the same time, I was going through a very hard financial crisis, and minutes before, I was debating with my wife, if we should miss our scheduled monthly mortgage payment—and some other credit card payments. He did not see me—but I kept on rolling my eyes, when he was talking on the phone—because his problems to me were so absurd—but I know, my problems for somebody who had a loved one in the hospital, would be irrational. I believe in the story, that the rooms of hospitals have heard more honest prayers—than the rooms of any temple. If you think you have a lot of problems, other than health, just visit somebody in the hospital—then you will realize having good health is the most important. A popular story of challenging hardship in life is, the life story of beloved President Lincoln. In his life before he became President, he lost eight elections, twice failed in business— and suffered a nervous breakdown. After all that hardship at the age of 52, he was inaugurated as the 16th President of the U.S.A. In addition to his oppressive life he suffered a personal tragedy, when his dear sister died at only 21 years old—also his sweetheart girlfriend died at young age. Probably the most devastating for him was—when two of his sons had died, of illness, only a couple years apart. Till the moment he was assassinated, he never gave up fighting for himself, and his family. He left a huge legacy, in his relatively short life.

102.

You might say: "Those people that left a huge legacy are special, they were born like that," which is not true. Hard work is everything. Talent is very important—but talent without hard work, or practice, becomes average. It is credited to Einstein—that he said: "Everyone is a genius. But if you judge a fish by its ability to climb a tree, it will live its whole life believing that it is stupid," even though there is no certainty Einstein has said it—but regardless who said it, it is a marvelous quote. Except talent and hard work, we have to concentrate on the things we like—and things we are capable of doing. A few years ago—my family and me—were big fans of American Idol, a singing competition TV show. Every season, there would be somebody, who clearly could not sing, but their family insisted that they were good—their family actually made them look like that fish trying to climb the tree. I am sure, they were good at some other things in life—but singing was definitely not it. Even with extra hard work—it was obvious they would never become famous singers—thus their family was leading them in the wrong direction. We must keep it real, and find the things we are good at—then hard work comes to be of the great service. Remember, we have just one life, and we are in control of it, and have to make sure to experiment, and discover, what we are good at. The worst thing is to listen to naysayers—I grew up in Balkans, that part of the world is famous, for having a lot of naysayers—and actually, they are so aware of it, they even make a lot of jokes about it. Usually, those naysayers would tell you something like: "Oh no, you cannot do it, forget about it, who you think you are, you are not too good, only lucky succeed, that is too hard, etc." And yes, it is very hard for people to succeed, if they constantly listen to naysayers—but we have to break free, and take the risk. A simple example is, let's say, a married man had to ask his wife at one point to marry him, and there are some unmarried guys that would like to be married—but were too scared to ask. The simple rule for everything is—if we don't ask for it—we don't get it. That is the same with the legacy, if we don't try—we will never achieve it. We should not be scared of rejection, and failure—because for most things in our life—we have to strive.

103.

There was this story, I heard some time back, of Dashrath Manjhi—he died a few years ago, but will be remembered for a long time. He lived in small village, in northeastern India, and was poor—but that did not intercept him to leave a legacy. In 1960, his wife was injured, and she died because of a lack of medical attention, due to the fact that his village was isolated by a mountain—which made it hard to reach the hospital in time. Soon after, he decided to buy a hammer, and chisel, and began chipping a stone, to make a cut through a hill. It took him over 20 years, to successfully complete his task, where he carved a 360 feet long path—in the stone. In the end, he shortened the way between two towns, from about 32 miles, to about 9 miles. Afterwards, his great achievement was recognized, and it was proposed that the road, and the small hospital be named after him. This story teaches us, that we don't need money to leave a legacy, all we need is will. It is never too late to succeed. Also, just a few weeks ago there was a story, on many major TV networks, about Harriette Thompson, a North Carolina lady, who became the oldest women to finish a marathon, thus far—at the age of 92. Her life was filled with many obstacles, including her fight with cancer, in two occasions, which she had to overcome. Being classically trained as a pianist—she played three times at Carnegie Hall, during her life. The media quoted her words—that the piano pieces she had performed, helped her mentally get through the 26.2 miles run. I mentioned these last two stories—just to indicate, that ordinary people of the world can leave a large legacy. It proves, that we don't need to be rich, or young, to leave something—that the world will remember us for. Then again, we don't have to wait until old age to do something extraordinary—due to the fact, that we might not live that long.

104.

I was planning on writing this book for a long time, and was always, telling myself "you are young you'll do it later." Just around last winter, I Googled, out of curiosity—to see how many people that decided to write a book, actually proceed to write it. The answer will surprise you—author Chris Guillebeau says that only 1% of people that plan to write a book complete the task. I told myself, this is it I want to be in that one percent. Even though, I was planning to write it soon, regardless, I started immediate plans to take time off from my job—and promised myself, to finish it during this summer of 2015. I pledged to myself to publish this book before my kids are out of high school, so hopefully they can take it with them to college. One year ago it sounded totally unrealistic to take time off from work, mostly because of all the bills—that are keeping me as their prisoner. I convinced myself—you can do it. That is all it takes, we have to make up our mind. Life goes so quickly, it seems to me like my children were just born yesterday—and that is what happens to most people. We always wait for the day we are off from work, to do things, or a vacation to try to relax, we people are always waiting for something. When it gets cold we look forward to the warm days, and when it gets warm we look forward to the cooler weather; always looking forward to something. When we make up our mind, and figure out what we want, everything clicks together. We have to put all the pieces together—and learn from our life's experiences, what our purpose in this world is, and act as soon as possible—please don't leave it for later. Remember everyone has a purpose in this life. Your purpose can come on its own—like in the case of the hero, when you fulfill your life's meaning, sometimes even without realizing it at first—but if it does not come like that—we have to search for it, and earn something, that our life will be remembered for. We have to give our own life the meaning.

105.

I will mention now, some of the heroes that have saved many lives. Heroism of Irena Sandler, during World War 2 is outstanding. Her father, Stanislaw Krzyzanowski probably made a huge influence on her—when she was a child. As a Polish physician in the early twentieth century, he was treating mostly poor Jewish people, and in the outbreak of typhus in 1917, he continued his good work, as a doctor—but eventually contracted the disease himself, and subsequently died from typhus—the same year. Irena inherited being a good person from her father, and during WW2—she was a nurse, and a social worker—in Poland. She was a Catholic, but devoted her life to help Jewish people in need—as should every normal human being do—help the people in need, regardless of their religion. Irena became a member of Zegota, which was a Polish Council to Aid Jews. She was very active in saving babies from the Warsaw Ghetto—which was like a large prison for Jewish people. As an employee of the Social Welfare Department, she was allowed to enter the Ghetto, to check for signs of any disease—because Germans were scared it would spread through the city. With the help of other Zegota members, she was able to smuggle approximately 2500 children outside the Ghetto—with the children's parent's approval. Kids were sheltered in the families outside the Ghetto—and she kept all records of babies, in a glass jars buried into the ground—so the kids could be reunited with their parents after the war. But, after the war, it was realized that many of the parents were killed—which would also most likely have been the case with the kids—if they had stayed in the Ghetto. It took many years after the war before people recognized her heroism. Inside of her, she knew that she did the right thing, and luckily she has lived to be 98 years old—and died knowing that she fulfilled her life's mission. It seems to me lately, that every time I read any news—I keep on getting to the stories of people sending messages to the world. Messages of hope, messages that tell us—there are so many heroes from whom we need to learn—and try to be like them. The great thing is—that with the Internet, we can learn of people, who have done, or are doing, those good things. James Harrison's story was published on many big news networks—all over the Internet. This great Australian started donating blood in 1954, as an eighteen year old. It was discovered, that his blood contains an unusually strong—and persistent antibody, which can help babies—who otherwise, would be at the risk of getting a deadly hemolytic disease of the newborn. With the donation of his blood plasma—that treats pregnant women, it is estimated that he saved over two million baby lives—thus far. He is my hero—same as Irena.

106.

I can make this book very long, just mentioning what I have learned from the world's greatest teachers—but, because I don't want to make it too long—those were only a few—I had to mention. There are many, many more authors of superb knowledge—that I adore. As for people that I have mentioned, which have reached their purpose in life—they were just like us, ordinary people. None of the people I mentioned, had any idea that they will make the world a better place, when they were in their early childhood; they had no idea that they would be remembered. Their life is a success; because they lived by moral and ethical rules. I can write pages, and pages about celebrities—many of them, as I said, took their status for granted—and just some have

recognized the gift they got. There is no need for more examples—
you have gotten the idea, you got my point—I am sure.

107.

We have to give meaning to our life. Life, which is lived without any
legacy left behind—is a wasted life. Nobody will remember us, ever.
I am sure—that on an everyday basis, at least a few million people
quote Aristotle. Why? Because, even though he lived twenty four
millenniums ago, he has left so much of a legacy—that his ideas will
live as long as the human race is existing. How about our average friend,
who will remember him or her? Most likely nobody. Disappointedly,
that is true. I am sorry to say that, but most people, will most likely,
end up being just a number to fill up statistics—just like trees. We
can do better. We have to try hard, to leave something that the world
will remember us for. I do not want us to kill ourselves by trying—of
course—and if we see that we are not capable of flying plains, or
navigating boats—we should not do those tasks. We have to find
something, that we are good at—like song writing, painting, science,
math, even walking across the continents, something remarkable,
something that the world will remember us—for forever. Remember,
be safe, give your best—and discover what you are good at. That is
the secret to life. Think about it. Even if you don't get recognition
for it, while you are alive—think of Tesla's words, "The present is
theirs; the future, for which I really worked, is mine." If you did
something extraordinary in your life, and in your opinion did not get
recognition—make those words be your motto. Just stay good—don't
let anything disappoint you. If you excelled in something, sooner or
later it will get recognition—remember, "What goes around comes
around." That is why I think Jesus was a very good man. It took
many years, before he was awarded with full recognition of being
a special person—and now millions of people mention his name,
on an everyday basis—same thing goes for Prophet Muhammad,

or Buddha. The problem sometimes is—that people don't follow exactly what those amazing individuals have said. Keep on doing the right things—think of Mahatma Gandhi, Nelson Mandela or Malala Yousafzai. Be like: Deepak Chopra, Wayne Dyer, Oprah Winfrey, Arnold Palmer, Louise Hay, Andrew Carnegie, or Bill Gates. Think of Victor Hugo's words: "People do not lack strength, they lack will." Life is never easy—life is a challenge that we have to accept—and give our best try to succeed. Just one life we have—and remember: The Secret to life—is to give your life a meaning. Do something great with your life. Be good.

BOOK ON RELIGION

1.

Hominins showed early signs, which could be interpreted as religion today. The cave paintings, possibly, were connected to some form of religion—hence some paintings of half-human, half-animal were found. Early religion was probably connected to the burial process. Some indication could be found in the Balkan Peninsula, in Krapina— which is part of Croatia now-days. That site is where Neanderthals buried their own, along with stone tools and animal bones. Graves were shallow, but still show the evidence of possible religious ritual— and it association of emotional connection to deceased. Except for the Krapina site, there are a few other Neanderthal burial sites—found mostly in the Middle East. Same as with history, once the first religious written texts appeared, from that time we consider—that religious history started. As mentioned in the first part of this book—Egyptian burial texts are considered among the oldest religious writings to exist. Writing definitely helped to spread organized religion—which proved pivotal later, when monotheistic Holy books had appeared. Once communication started, early people invented worshiping different things. Quite a few different systems have been developed.

2.

Polytheism is the belief in many Gods, and it is believed, that it started with Hinduism. There are many Gods present in their religion, even though, I have heard it myself, from some Hindu friends—that they technically believe in one supreme God, Brahma. Later, as we know other cultures developed polytheism—including Babylonia, Assyria, Egypt, and of course Greece, and Rome. The last two developed a highly structured pantheon of the Gods, and Goddesses. Pantheism, which was a belief that all is a God—developed a little bit later, in Pharaohs Egypt, Buddhism, Confucianism, Taoism, and other cultures of the Far East—and also in some African, and Native American cultures. Their main principle is that God is everything, and everything is God—including nature, of course. Monotheism, is the belief in one God, and it is the foundation of the Jewish, Christian, and Muslim religion—that started with the Prophet Abraham (Abram, Avram or Ibrahim). In that belief system, God revealed himself—to human individuals, or Angels, apparently. Nowadays, Monotheism is the largest religion system—that has spread all around the world. Lately, some of the religious philosophies are getting noticeable recognition—like in the case of Deism, where people believe in the one God, that created the universe—but reject religious books that claim to contain revealed word of God, religious dogma, demagogy, and reports of miracles. Another philosophy that is gaining huge number of followers is Atheism—which has total absence of any belief—that any Deities exist.

3.

It is interesting to learn, that in many religions, there is the belief that God, or Gods had possible intercourse—with human ladies. It was considered normal, that nice ladies were happy about it—and woman's consent was taken for granted. I will mention, with all due respect a few examples; apparently Hindu God Shiva—who had two wives already, at one point was making love with a human lady Madhura, as told in Ramayana; or Greek God Zeus—who made son Hercules with a human lady. According to the Buddhist tradition, Buddha's mother Maya—who was human, was married to a human King Suddhodhana—and got pregnant with deity. The King and Queen did not have children for twenty years into their marriage—and suddenly Queen Maya finds herself pregnant with the future Buddha—after she was entered from the side—by the God, in the dream. Probably the most popular story of God, and human combination—was told in the two gospels of the New Testament—in the Christian Bible. Not in all four, but in two. Gospel of Luke, and Gospel of Matthew, told us the story of Jesus' birth, where his mother Mary who was married to Joseph—but still was a virgin. Christians strongly believe, that Jesus' mother was impregnated—by the spirit of the Lord. Interesting story, is all I can say.

4.

It usually comes to, where you were born, to which religion you will belong. Especially, let's say, fifty years ago—if you were born in Italy, most likely you would be Catholic, or Saudi Arabia, almost definitely Muslim—or in America, your chances to be Protestant Christian were the highest. Also, if you were born in a different region, most likely, you would adopt the religion of your parents. In some cases, if the kid or kids did not want to continue the family tradition of a certain religion, their family, would cut all ties with them—in some cases. I believe, many times for that reason, because of fear, kids continued with the family's religion. In my case, I was born in the Christian dominant Austria, to the parents of Bosnian Muslims. They were not radical Muslims, but observed Muslim holy-days. My Father paid a lot of money, for me to be born, in one of the best Hospitals in

Vienna—St. Anna Kinderspital. I am pretty sure my birth hospital is named after St. Anna, the grandmother of Jesus. My first, and last name, are very Muslim. Erol is a Turkish name for brave or leader; and both of my parents liked that name. My last name is from my ancestors. First part, Hafiz, is actually like a title, which is given to the person—that has memorized the whole book of Qur'an—which I guess some of my great grandfathers did. The second part is begović, which means son of the bey (beg)—and that is a title too. Beg is an old Turkish word, and was given as a title, to a leader—or a governor of the province—in the Ottoman Empire; or in some cases it was a title for a chieftain of the tribal group. As far as I know—my first, and last name, are fairly common in Bosnia—but I am the only person in the whole world—with this first and last name combination. I love the history, and I am proud of my name. Anyways, as a kid I remember seeing my father pray home—more often than my mom. I don't think they prayed in the mosque, as far as I know. In my personal case, I never prayed inside any kind of Temple, ever. More importantly, I was constantly told to believe in God—and to be good to everyone, regardless of their religion. I was also constantly told to be good in general, to respect others, and never commit a crime—which I think I have succeeded with, thus far. And that is my motto—be good. That is all I keep on telling my kids now—be good.

5.

When I moved to America, I was expecting it to be an all Christian nation. Later, I had learned that the Founding Fathers that wrote the Constitution, and Amendments, actually agreed not to mention Christianity, Jesus, or God, anywhere. As a matter of fact, religion in general is mentioned only two times. In the First Amendment it says: "Congress shall make no law respecting an establishment of religion, or prohibiting the free exercise thereof; or abridging the freedom of speech, or of the press, or the right of the people peaceably to assemble....," and in Article VI, third paragraph: "The Senators and Representatives before mentioned, and the Members of the several State Legislatures, and all executive and judicial Officers, both of the United States and of the several States, shall be bound by Oath or Affirmation, to support this Constitution; but no religious Test shall ever be required as a Qualification to any Office or public..." I remember learning a lot about U.S. history, when I had to pass the test for U.S. Citizenship—over 12 years ago. The bottom line is, that the Founding Fathers wanted respect for all—and gradually religious pluralism became the norm. It is nice to see religious freedom all across America. I have driven people to Churches, as well as Mosques, Synagogues, and Hindu Temples—many times. As a matter of fact, every day I drive by different Temples, and I see happy faces. I am a witness—that people in America can follow any religion they want. Thanks to the Founding Fathers.

6.

Even though I do not attend any religious services, or visit any religious Temple—for the reason of praying inside—I respect people that are doing it. Everybody has a right to believe in whatever they want. As I mentioned, in the first part of the book—I believe in God, but not as the old Man sitting in the clouds; my God is Universal Energy—that Supreme Power, which is in charge. I possibly consider it as a male, because energy is a vigor—and vigor I consider in the male form, even though energy has no gender. Anyway, every time I pray, I call that Vigor—the Dear God. Ever since I was little, I pray every single day. I pray inside myself, mostly in Bosnian— and occasionally, in English. I think, everybody should pray in the language they understand, not in the language of their religion, unless they understand that language. I ask Dear God to help me go through the day without any problems. I do not think, that there is a personal God—which just hangs around—and sometimes says, "oops I had not heard you that time," if something bad happens. It is more like, when we say a prayer—it is recorded in some sort of invisible cloud, personal cloud that follows us everywhere—I believe that cloud is the part of the Ether. As Ether is very active area, it has that invisible cloud—and everything else is recorded in there. It is good to pray for future things too, like ask for a good fortune, future husband, or wife, kids, etc. Just imagine it, give your wish a life—make it exist. As I mentioned before, the whole Universe is built of the same matter. People, and the whole Universe—as well as the God, are made of the same chemical elements. Someone's wishes may come true, regardless if they pray to Jesus, Allah, Ganesh, Yahweh, any Saint, Buddha, your imaginary deity, or even if you are Atheist—as long as your wish is good and reasonable. If you can absorb the power from the Energy— your wish will possibly be granted. We, citizens of the world are all equal, we might have cultural differences—but deep inside we are all the same, period.

7.

Dear God treating us all equally, and receiving our prayers equally, regardless who you address it to—as long as you are a good person. Your requirement is to ask for it—and to be good. You should work to support you and your family, help others, donate extra money, volunteer if possible, leave a legacy, and be happy. That's why you have happy and healthy people in all different cultures, regardless of their religion. Many years ago, in New York, one of my fellow drivers—who was not Christian, by the way—told me, while we were waiting for a pick up: "Look at all these wealthy Christians, maybe their religion is the best, they have all these big houses and all this stuff." My answer was: "Go to Dubai or Kuwait, and see how many rich Muslim people live there, or in New Delhi you'll see many rich Hindu people over-there." Anywhere you go you'll see wealthy people, regardless of their religion, or their culture; more important than what religion, or culture

you belong, is to do good things, all of the time. You can learn about
that when you travel around the world, because if you stay just in one
place all the time, you'll think that your religion is the best in the whole
world. Ignorance is very dangerous. If you don't learn of the other
religions, and cultures, you cannot understand them either. Maybe you
are just stubborn, and feel comfortable in what you believe in already,
even though, what you believe in might be one hundred percent a
myth, but it's okay—it's a free world—and you have the free will to
believe in anything you want. As said before, what goes around comes
around—it is a life's rule—regardless to who you pray to, your chances
are equal to succeed; as long as you are a good person. Be good—that
is true religion. Of course, I know that bad things happen to good
people too, regardless of what religion they belong to, or how much
they have prayed. Sometimes, some good people are too good, and
naïve. We have to be good to a certain level—but if somebody tries to
take advantage of us—in that case we have to make a cut—because
if somebody uses us as a fool, we can get killed or injured. We have to
be good, but we should definitely never let anybody abuse us. Also,
we don't know what the deceased person was thinking about, maybe
they were the kindest person around, but they were thinking too much
about death and dying. In my opinion—if you think too much, and
too hard, about death and dying it can become a reality; that is the
Law of Attraction—which I will address more in the "Wealth" part
of this book. Again, with thinking you create life, depending on how
strong your connection is with Universal Energy—you might be able
to initiate something to happen. Thus, for that reason, be careful what
you are thinking about. If you do all the right things, and pray for a
good fortune, even if something bad happens to you, you will feel better
knowing that you did all you can do—you will feel more peaceful.

8.

I believe if you did, or said, something wrong it could be fixed—but it will not be as easy, as some religions try to make you believe. There are a few different types of acknowledgements of the wrong-doings. I believe that your confession of doing something wrong is helpful, because you have realized your wrong-doing, and will try to fix it. Forgiveness can be granted only by the Dear God, or partly also by a harmed individual—and under no circumstances, it could be granted to you by a third party. Depending on how bad your wrong-doing was, it can definitely make a difference. If you did something wrong, and have caused loss, pain, or suffering to someone—your best option is to admit it, and at the Court of Law try to defend yourself. If you were given jail time, accept it and do your time, it will help you feel free after your release from the jail. Don't forget to apologize to the harmed party also. However, if you honestly did not commit the crime, and still have gotten the jail time—then try to fight it with the appeal. If you still have to do jail time after the appeal—be peaceful, and believe, that you are collecting good points for your afterlife. Some things you cannot change, but truth is recorded and exist in the Ether also. Coming back to that word, Ether in Physics is "a hypothetical substance supposed to occupy all space, postulated to account for the propagation of electromagnetic radiation through space," according to dictionary.com; and I agree with that, and I am adding again—that Ether also acts as something like a hard drive, to store all of the things we do—as well as—it is the new home for the deceased. Everything that is not physical lives in Ether.

9.

Doing something wrong, and then trying to get forgiveness through religious confession, does not work. It reminds me of a story, which could be a legend, I have heard a long time ago; about the boy—who went to his family's religious temple, where "he learned to pray all the time, and he was told that if he wants something just to pray for it, and it will be given to you." He also learned—that if he did something wrong, he can be forgiven for his wrong-doing—if he makes the confession. So, boy prayed and prayed for a toy he wished to have—but his prayers did not work for him; and he had never gotten the toy. One day, after he learned of confession, he considered to steal the toy, and then ask for forgiveness through confession—and possible thief was born. I have a feeling that this story was based on the true story; some people knowingly do some bad things counting on the confession. Well, it does not work like that, if you do something wrong—you have to pay for it. In the case the harmed individual can forgive you for the damage you will be partly free of guilt, but if you did something very wrong—the harmed individual forgiveness cannot help you. We can be partly forgiven also by asking for forgiveness from the Universal Energy, deep from the heart, and it can help us some. In my opinion, best way to get more forgiveness from Universal God—is if you commit yourself on doing only good things—for the rest of your life. That could be obtained through constant meaningful help to people in need—by different means, like: Volunteering in the hospitals, libraries, retirement homes, parks, etc. Some religions used to accept money as a form of indulgence. I am sure that money cannot buy you forgiveness; if you did something wrong and have the money, then go to the poor areas of the world, buy things for the needed—by yourself only, not through the third party. Commit yourself on saving lives, but remember, you have to commit yourself to it from the heart—that is the only way to gain the forgiveness.

10.

I think, that having all different religious Temples is a positive thing in general—for the reason that many people would go to sleep hungry;

if they did not receive their meal from their place of worship. Also, many religious places of worship financially help the poor. As long as they stay in that domain—everything is fine. Many times, certain religious Temples start growing so rapidly, their leaders lose the original point. With the money donations, that their Temple collects, Temple's high officials start buying expensive cars, extra-large houses, jewelry, even airplanes for themselves. I believe, Jesus was a humble man, very modest, courteously respectful, and if he lived nowadays there is no way he would have a craving for those material things—I have a feeling he would own something like a Ford Focus (here I give the respect to Pope Francis—who occasionally is driven in one). I also think, the good man Jesus is very upset about many things that were done in his name. Religion made him get huge respect in one hand—but in the other, religious leaders used him for their benefit. Through my work, as I said before, many times I have driven people to many different religious Temples—and many times, I transported workers of the Temples. One time, there was a big convention of one of the most popular Christian denominations in America. Leaders of their churches had luxury car transportation, and I had these two gentleman—that sat in the back seat of my car. Of course, they started comparing, and talking about their churches—because they were located in different areas. All I heard, while I transported them to the hotel was: "How many...how much...money...money...," not even once, did either gentleman say anything like—it is good to have people to believe. In this case, believers were just numbers—and I am worried, that it is becoming more, and more—like a pattern. After I dropped them off at the hotel, I had opened all the windows in my car, because their energy was pretty heavy to handle. I had realized, that believing has turned into business. Also, many people, which attend the religious services, believe literally—in everything they hear. Many times I have discussed religion with my fellow drivers—and many of them strictly believe, into whatever was written in their holy book. To me, they seem like they would die to protect every single word they read, or were told. I had a fellow driver in New York, who was "sure," that the world started with Jesus Christ, and he told me "but the calendar proves that world started with Jesus Christ." Also, another time in Orlando I asked a fellow driver—who I think is a good man—"how come you could believe that the world is only six thousand years old? Is it because Christianity claims that?" In addition, I told him that I respect his deep Christian belief—but I wanted to know if he understands all the scientific evidence. He looked me—as I was from another planet—and said: "You have no idea, six thousand years is a lot of time." It was the end of conversation for me.

11.

Occasionally, I find myself watching Christian channels on my TV. In my experience, I have felt, that there is always first a little bit of threatening; "if you don't accept Jesus, you'll go to hell," or "you have sins," and then a little bit later: "Make a donation, now." I have gotten the feeling, that using the word "sin," or the name "Lord" is crucial—for getting donations. The interesting thing is, that people keep on sending them the money—I try to believe, that some people who did, or are doing wrong things in life, are assured, that they are buying excuses for their wrong-doings with donations they make—as I said above, it does not work, and it is nonsense. Monetary donations will not help them—if they are evil people. I also understand TV guys, that's their job—they have no other way to make money. Another example I have learned through my job, is that some people in the Middle East—really have a lot of money. If you explore, you will learn, that there are hundreds of members of Saudi Royal family. King Ibn Saud had estimated hundred kids—and many of those kids have many of their own, each. I had realized that—after I had transported a few different Princes and Princesses—in a short period of time. The good thing for my company, city, and country of the U.S.A., is that they are spending unimaginable amounts of money—but is it moral for them to do that? One time, I picked up one Princess, that reserved a car, and a van for transportation to a private airplane—it turned out, that she liked shopping—and had 39 loaded pieces of expensive luggage. We finally left the hotel with my car—and the other three vans. After that transport, I kept on thinking all day about all the hungry kids—all around the world, who would be happy just to get—at least one meal per day. I don't think—that neither Jesus, nor Prophet Muhammed, would approve of the waste of money—that is happening today. Don't get me wrong, I am not against shopping, and buying good quality items—but I think we all should know when to stop.

12.

I love Mother Teresa—if anybody has fulfilled their meaning in life, it was her. It shows, you can be a Catholic Nun, and leave a wonderful legacy. Her birth name was Anjeze Gonxhe Bojaxhiu, and she was born in the Balkan's area—same as my other favorite person, Nikola Tesla. Both of them knew how to speak the same language as me— and I feel good about that. She left home at an early age, to help poor people in India. First, she was a teacher in Loreto convent school, sometime after, she was very disturbed by the surrounding poverty, and started the mission to care—in her own words, for: "The hungry, the naked, the homeless, the crippled, the blind, the lepers, all those people who feel unwanted, unloved, uncared for throughout society, people that have become a burden to the society and are shunned by everyone." After seeing suffering individuals, she decided to dedicate her life to helping others. First, she opened the Home for Dying in 1952, and a home for those who suffered from leprosy, in 1955. That lovely lady kept on going opening many missions, encouraged by attracting many recruits, and charitable donations. According to CNN—in 1982, she even came to Beirut, and in the middle of the war she rescued 37 children—by negotiating temporary cease-fire. In her life she received many awards, and in 1979 Mother Teresa was awarded the Nobel Peace Prize "for work undertaken in the struggle to overcome poverty and distress, which also constitutes as a threat to peace." She asked, that the monetary award funds be given to the poor people—in India. When she was receiving the prize, she was asked: "What can we do to promote world peace?"—she answered: "Go home and love your family." The meaning of life, well done!

13.

If I had to pick a theological doctrine, that I think is right for the most part—I would give advantage to the Deist approach to God. The difference between Deists and me is, that I believe in some miracles—and they don't. I most definitely don't believe in any miracles from religious scriptures—but I believe in some life miracles I have witnessed myself. I have driven more than a million miles professionally—and have seen many bad accidents. It is amazing, that some people walk away unharmed, after being involved in a devastating car crash. I had a couple minor crashes my-self, but thanks to Dear God—I was saved many times. I had this situation in New York, when the car in front of me suddenly stopped on the highway—while cars were going at high speed. I still cannot explain how I did not hit him, or flip over. There was a special power that was turning my steering wheel, left and right in between many cars. We all avoided the crash—and I still think it was not me navigating. The person who I think definitely knew that, was the late Dan Osman. He was a Japanese American extreme sports practitioner, and was famous for rapid rock climbing—without any safety equipment. Dan made history with a free fall jump of 1000 feet from the mount cliff— while only being connected to safety rope. I watched many videos of him practicing his sports, and I watched him talk to the camera— little before he died, and after setting the record jump, he was giving credit to his Guardian Angels—that protect him, thus far. He felt the existence of Guardian Angels (which many religions also claim to exist); but the day he died, he probably had pushed too much—he really did not need those extra jumps. With the free will, we all have to recognize when to stop. In his recorded words he proved to me, that he knew what the meaning to life was—when in the same video he said "...book of world records is the mark of excellence in human achievement, and I am honored to be part of it..." I strongly believe, that there is that power that can protect us. That power is unseen— and we humans cannot make any communication with it. I agree that the best name to fit for that power is—Guardian Angels. You usually have to live an active life to feel their existence.

14.

Many people tried to fool the world, by claiming, that they are "mediums"; that they have supernatural gifts to communicate between humans, and spirits, of the live, and the dead people. I am convinced— it is impossible. As I said above—I believe we humans can feel the presence of the Guardian Angels, and other spirits—but nobody can make direct contact to them. The best magician in my opinion that has ever lived on Earth was Erik Weisz—or better known by the stage name as—Harry Houdini. Recently, I watched two TV series, starring Adrian Brody and Kristen Connolly—about Houdini's life, and since then—I like him even more. Houdini had spent a large part of his life fighting against "those" people, bad people—which were lying that they could communicate with the dead. I even have a feeling, that the fight against mediums—is what cost him to lose his life—in the end. While alive, he told his wife; who was his magic assistant too, that if it is possible, he will contact her from the afterlife. Apparently, that contact, in the way he explained to her that he will try, never happened. If anybody, in the history of humankind, would be able to find a way to communicate from afterlife—it would be Mr. Houdini. Another magician that I admire a lot is—James Randi, also known as the Amazing Randi—or in his own words "honest liar." Except his exceptional career as a magician, he devoted his life to debunking supernatural claims. I believe in his word, that mediums are just using magic, to fascinate, or to get money from the ordinary people—when they claim to have the power to communicate with the afterlife. I am big fan of his JREF Foundation, where he is offering a one million dollar reward, for anybody who can prove—anything supernatural. After many years, and many contestants for the prize, nobody has won that money yet—and I don't think anyone will win ever, in the future to come. I am assured that Mr. Randi definitely knows all the tricks, and I hope his followers, workers of his foundation, will continue his great job in the future.

15.

Magic is supposed to be the art of producing illusions for entertainment purposes, instead of being part of religion. Early religion was loaded with magic, and that was, in my opinion, the way to get more followers. Even, till just less than a couple of hundred years ago, witchcraft was a widespread belief in society—it was used in combination with religion, to have the social control. In many places, it was believed, that religious leaders were able to cure the illness—or even to improve the crop production. In 1856, Arabs of Algeria opposed French colonialists, and it was believed that they were ready to rebel against them. Napoleon III, had a great idea, to send great French magician Jean Eugene Robert-Houdin—to the rescue. Local Algerians were impressed by their leaders, who possibly used magic to control them; but Robert-Houdin was even better. Locals did not know that he used magic for the extraordinary things he did, and were so impressed, that even their leaders—who probably were thinking, that he had some of God's power—so, they started wearing red robes symbolizing their loyalty to France. Magic proved to be a powerful tool in controlling the masses—through their belief. Algerians were under the French rule for many more years to come, because of the magnificent Robert-Houdin and his magic. As you probably know, Harry Houdini took his stage name to honor Robert-Houdin—but later in the life Harry did not like him much. I love magic—and I think magic is amazing. Every time I watch magic tricks, live or on TV, I get amazed at how good some magicians are. Five years ago we watched one magic show live, in Las Vegas, and I happened to be right there in the front row—a few feet away from the performers. I concentrated myself to see if I could figure out how they do it. This couple was dancing right in front of my eyes—and the lady was switching dresses from short to long, and back to short—in all different colors. I was close enough to notice that there was not multiple layers of dresses on her, and I still have no idea how they did it. Simply amazing, as long as it stays as a show, and not the religion.

16.

Early rituals of sacrifice were influenced heavily by magic. Monotheistic religions did a great job fighting against different blood sacrifices—which were common in pagan beliefs. Sacrifice rituals, were part of life in the Babylonian, Persian, Aztec, and Maya's civilizations. It was hard for monotheistic religions to totally eliminate sacrifices. In the beginning Jewish traditions were practicing sacrifice, as they learned in Torah, but it is believed that with the destruction of the Temple in Jerusalem—which was the only place to do it—now there was no need to do it anymore. Islam still continues the practice of sacrifice, which could be a cow, goat, sheep, or some other animal—to honor God for not killing Ibrahim's son. In Islam, Prophet Ibrahim was willing to sacrifice his own son (same as in Judaism and Christianity), but was advised by God, through the Angel, not to kill the boy. Christians adopted the belief that Jesus was sacrificed for everyone's sake, so there is no need for additional sacrifices.

17.

According to the American Humanist official website: "Humanism is a progressive life stance that, without supernaturalism, affirms our ability and responsibility to lead meaningful, ethical lives capable of adding to the greater good of humanity." It is based on the ethical values that include critical thinking. Most Humanists prefer scientific evidence, over religious dogma. Humanist philosophy mostly matches my view on life except—that most humanist movements typically don't believe in God, and the afterlife—and even though, there are a few different branches of Religious Humanism—our views don't match exactly. Many members of the Humanist movement are very good people, and many dedicate their life to helping others; and support everyone's individual liberty, and maintain dignity of each human being. Humanists protect human rights—and push for social justice. With helping others in mind, many humanists, are philanthropists too. As a matter of fact, the word philanthropy, is derived from Greek—and literally means "love of humanity," which makes all of the philanthropists partly Humanist. In my opinion the world needs more people like that.

18.

Growing up, I had heard hundreds of times, from friends and family that everyone has a destiny; and that everything, including everyone's life, is determined. As a kid, I actually took that almost for granted. It is actually very common, especially in the Balkan area, to use that phrase; "It's all determined." In my search for the meaning of life, I have spent a lot of time thinking about that, and came to a conclusion— that things in life are not all determined. I strongly believe, that we humans have a free will, and that we can decide, in most cases, what to do—unless we lose our mind, or are under some drug influence.

The only time when something is determined, is when people keep on doing the same mistake—then they will be determined to fail, like the old saying "who plays with a gun will die from the gun," it's the same with everything else. If you realize that you are going into a wrong direction, stop, and you will not be determined to fail, or die. The thing that upsets me the most is, when people knowingly do something wrong, and then blame it on something else—or when they expect to get free things—like they are entitled to it, without work. I am pretty sure, that everyone had a situation in their life, when they were influencing their life, with their own decisions—for better or worse. If I did not work hard, as I have been, my family would not have a nice house—and would not have the opportunity to travel to all of the different places—that we have traveled to. I could have worked less, or even applied for welfare, as being a legal resident—but I never did. If I followed that "determined" idea—I probably, would have not even written this book. I made myself do it. As adults, many people, myself included, had the situation to cheat. I had to fight with myself—I told myself NO, just do the right thing. At those moments, I had won a big battle of life—and that win is for the better. I have learned a huge lesson, to be better prepared for next time. A couple of times, I think even my Guardian Angels helped me—because I was at the verge of making a mistake, and they had stopped it—I give them credit for it. In life, it takes just a moment to act wrong, to make a mistake, and possibly, regret it for your whole life. Many times, there are two or more opportunities, like intersections on the road, and we don't need to go to the shiny looking one. Sometimes what looks more is less—what looks shinier can actually turn out to be very unpleasant. Experience is essential. Always in life do the right thing, and be good.

19.

If you ask an average person—who they think Albert Einstein was, the answer most likely would be: A physicist. I believe, that he is most famous for developing the general theory of relativity, and in popular culture, his mass-energy equivalence formula $E = mc^2$ has a legendary status. In 1921, he had received a Nobel Prize for his work in physics. I am sure—that mostly everyone will agree, that Mr. Einstein was one of the smartest people that ever lived on Earth. For a big part of my life, I also connected Einstein to physics only—but in the search for the meaning, I have discovered, that he wrote a lot about his opinion of religion, and God. While he was still living in Germany, he received a telegram from prominent American Rabbi Herbert S. Goldstein, asking him if he believed in God. Einstein replied, in German: "I believe in Spinoza's God, who reveals himself in the harmony of all that exists, not in a God who concerns himself with the fate and doings of mankind." Baruch Spinoza was a Dutch philosopher, who lived in the seventeen century—and he had laid the foundation for modern biblical criticism. His views on God were criticized by the Jewish community, where he belonged at first. Right after he died, at the age of 44, his most popular book Ethics was published. The fundamental principle of Ethics is—that God is the natural world, literally God is Nature, and Nature is God. As mentioned earlier, that view is Pantheism—and even though, that word came to use after his death—his work most likely influenced the idea. Neither Einstein, nor Spinoza—believed in a personal God. German Jewish philosopher Eric Gutkind wrote the book Choose Life: The Biblical Call to Revolt, and had sent the copy to Einstein, to see his opinion. Einstein had sent Gutkind a letter in response—and wrote: "The word God is for me nothing more than the expression and product of human weaknesses, the Bible a collection of honorable, but still primitive legends. No interpretation no matter how subtle can (for me) change this. These subtilized interpretations are highly manifold according to their nature and have almost nothing to do with the original text." Einstein disassociated himself from being called an atheist either, and thought more of himself as agnostic, for a reason that he believed in God—which human nature is limited to experience.

20.

Both Spinoza, and Einstein held a philosophical position of determinism. That doctrine believes that all events are determined by causes, and that it has nothing to do with our will; human action as being part of it, made some people believe that they cannot be held responsible for their actions. With that idea—I strongly disagree. Spinoza had a totally opposite belief then one of my favorite teachers, French philosopher Rene Descartes—who I have mentioned in the Introduction section of this book. Many people believe, that Descartes has set the foundation for all knowledge, with the statement "I think, therefore I am." I also support Descartes idea, that body and mind are two separate entities—that was the foundation for Spinoza's criticism of Descartes. Einstein sided with Spinoza, and it was recorded that he said: "I am fascinated by Spinoza's Pantheism. I admire even more his contributions to modern thought. Spinoza is the greatest of modern philosophers, because he is the first philosopher who deals with the soul and the body as one, not as two separate things," and in Einstein's book The World As I See It—he wrote the paragraph: "I cannot conceive of a God who rewards and punishes his creatures, or has a will of the type of which we are conscious in ourselves. An individual who should survive his physical death is also beyond my comprehension, nor do I wish it otherwise; such notions are for the fears or absurd egoism of feeble souls. Enough for me the mystery of the eternity of life, and the inkling of the marvelous structure of reality, together with the single-hearted endeavor to comprehend a portion, be it never so tiny, of the reason that manifests itself in nature." The bottom line is, that I have to agree with Descartes, that body and soul can be separated. I also agree with Spinoza, that God is everything, and everything is God—which makes sense—but I still think, that we have to be responsible for our actions. After a long time of thinking about what is going to happen with us in the afterlife; I believe that the soul will depart the body, and will continue to live while the body will decay. In many near-death experience stories, everyone who came back, agrees with one thing; that they have left their physical body, and observed what is happening around their motionless body. I believe that it is the first phase after death.

21.

In 2011, the Population Reference Bureau estimated—that almost 108 billion of modern humans—ever lived on Earth. I used their data in the first part of the book too—but their numbers for the world population are approximate—because they started their count from the year 50,000 BCE; and modern humans probably evolved earlier than that—but they had to start the count from somewhere. Regardless, I am very thankful for their data. Even if I take approximate numbers, and divide it with a current estimate of people living on Earth today, I come to the conclusion, that there are 14 to 16 dead people on every one living person on the Earth—living now. I believe that all those souls are still in the Ether. You might think that, it is way too many souls, and the skies must be overcrowded—but I don't think so. Philosophy of René Descartes holds that the mind is a nonphysical substance, and I am thinking that the mind is the soul, and mind is the one which leaves the body when we die—so that's why even without the body—we will remember everything from our physical life—when we die. According to Jefferson Lab (JLab), which is a U.S. National laboratory, a typical human of 70 kg, that is about 178lbs, contains almost $7*10^{27}$ atoms in the body. That is seven followed by twenty seven zeros. As I mentioned earlier, we are made of the same substance as the universe it-self; and according to JLab, from those seven billion, billion, billion atoms in our body, almost 2/3 are hydrogen atoms, 1/4 are oxygen, and about 1/10 are carbon atoms—which in total, those three groups of atoms add up to 99% of one human body. So, one average person contains trillions of atoms in their body, and let's say—that possibly soul is the size of the atom, which I am just imagining now—108 billion dead souls would fit in the hand of the average person.

22.

Those 14 to 16 dead people for every living—is still a low number, even if there were more people ever living, and we increase the number to 20—it is still not too high of a number. With the old religions they have felt the presence of souls around them, but had a feeling that only two advisers were around, good spirit, and evil spirit. After a long time of thinking I came to the conclusion, that we are followed by many more. Remember what I said earlier, we cannot communicate with them—but we can feel their presence. Just close your eyes now, and relax in a quiet room—after some time with your eyes closed think of somebody deceased, I am sure you will feel their presence—in the form of goose bumps. I am warning you not to do it too often, because you should not disturb them from their afterlife obligations to much—and also you can attract some spirits you don't really want. So, you have your own spirits that follow you everywhere—some are your Guardian Angels, and some will try to take you the wrong way. The ones that you make stronger connection with, will win—it is your decision to who you want to connect to more. Good spirits can help you, and even save you to a certain level—but if you abuse their help; let's say—by taking too many risks—you'll die too. Remember, you don't want to die before leaving a memorable legacy. Spirit power is limited, and remember, sometimes you'll have more good ones, and sometimes more bad ones, around you. The more good things you do, the more you'll attract smart and good souls that will help you in life. If you keep on breaking the law, bad souls will be your friends. Again, like attracts alike. Remember, the spirits of Einstein, or Jesus, are still around us. That is another reason to be good, all of the time. Naturally, I believe, that all of us, when we die will become spirits too, and this life we are living now is just a test, a challenge—to see what we will do with our life. Everyone has an equal opportunity; we cannot say "but it is all easy for rich people," because take the example of Mother Teresa, she did not have any money, or connections—but lived a life worth living. When we die, I believe, our soul in the form of the spirit, will be positioned according to our doings. Regardless of their religion, we all respect certain historic individuals, just for who they were; not because they believed in a certain religion. That shows us that it really makes no difference which religion you will pick—just be good person. I think, we all love and respect them, because they scored high on the afterlife's list—for the reason because they did extraordinary things while alive. They might have written beautiful music, painted a picture, won medals, helped somebody, or something else; but we celebrate them for who they were—not what religion they belonged to. The bigger the legacy you leave behind you—the higher you will be positioned in the afterlife, and if you were an honest and good person, I am sure you will be happy over there. I don't know how it looks like in the afterlife—but I am sure we will prefer to be with the good people—same as in this life. I don't think there is anybody who goes into prison, and enjoys it. Again, just do all good things, and I am sure you will be fine.

23.

Not just your visible works get recorded, but your thoughts too. There could be a person, that looks like a very good person, in the eyes of others—but inside that individual is mean, jealous, and had some dangerous thoughts. Evil thoughts will get you more evil spirits, and of course positive thoughts will attract good spirits. We have no idea what people are thinking around us, they might be very pleasant from outside—but inside they might pray for you to be hurt. I do not believe in exorcism, or any similar kind, of third party fighting with your spirits. Forget about Ouija boards, that's for unstable individuals, they are all fake—in my opinion. Remember again, absolutely no one human can make communication between people and spirits, period. You are the only one who can win this battle, remember this forever, only you. This is our own battle. If we feel the presence of bad spirits around us, by doing good and right things, we will force him or her to leave. For example, if you have a surge of need to steal something, don't do it. It will hurt you on the long term, and will get you more bad spirits. Every time you have an unexplainable need to do something wrong, don't do it. That is the only way to kick bad spirits far from you. Doing good, and moral things drives bad spirits insane—they will run away from you, like there is no tomorrow. Don't worry about bad spirits, they cannot hurt you physically—but will possibly make you hurt yourself, if you don't control yourself, and win the battle. They will just make your mind scared. Don't be weak, you have to fight with it yourself, and you have the power to win. By taking long walks, breathing deeply, and making plans to do good things—we will get rid of bad spirits, and attract good Energy—which will make us strong, and in control. We are all made of the same stuff—people, good spirits, bad spirits, and even Supreme Energy. Again saying, even though we live on Earth, which is like the smallest dot in the vast space of the Universe—we are still all connected to it.

24.

For your information, again, every single atom that ever existed on Earth is still present. Remember, the atoms of Aristotle, Tesla, Lincoln, Einstein, and all of the other great minds are still around us. Like the water you are drinking now, has been drunk by many people before. Everything in the Universe is made up of protons, neutrons, and electrons. Some elements are composed of a different combination, for example hydrogen is composed of one proton and one electron, carbon is composed of six protons, six neutrons and six elections, or helium is composed of two protons, two neutrons and two electrons. For the

Universe to exist as we know it—it is required for hydrogen to be converted into helium. Everything in the universe is synchronized, so for that reason—there has to be some Supreme Energy to keep things running smooth. That Power does not listen to personal stories—but it acts according to your doings. You decide your life, for better or worse. Like I said before, with praying you are collecting some of the positive Energy—but there are no guaranties that you will be able to receive it. If you do not concentrate on the prayer, you will not be strong enough to absorb that Energy. The more you get yourself into it, the more Energy you will absorb. Remember, that Supreme Energy is made of the same elements as you. The more you respect the Energy, and the more sincere you are from your heart—you will have a better chance of absorbing the Power. Simple as that.

25.

If you remember the story of Nikola Tesla, from the first part of this book; I said—that he was in the group of people that have discovered the meaning of life, in my opinion. I also think—he was searching for God, as much as, he was searching for new discoveries in his field of work. His father was actually Orthodox Christian priest, and probably, wanted Nikola to continue his steps—but, I am sure, Nikola did not listen to anyone—except to his inner self. He had spent countless hours in discoveries of many new ideas. When he said: "If you want to find the secrets of the universe, think in terms of energy, frequency and vibration," I have a feeling—that he was searching for God, and with the statement: "My brain is only a receiver, in the Universe there is a core from which we obtain knowledge, strength and inspiration. I have not penetrated into the secrets of this core, but I know that it exists," he definitely showed me, that we are talking about the same God.

26.

As religions were spreading across the globe, they all had very similar messages. They all claimed to be the best—and the only way to the better life, and afterlife. In one part of the world—one religion—and in the other part—another religion. When you look at it with a clear mind, it looks absurd. One of the key things is to scare followers—if they start walking away from their religion. In history, many times people switch between religions, and nothing happened to them. It shows that you only have to be good person, that's all. Even Spinoza's family was Jewish first, then Christian—and before he was born— they switched back to be Jewish again. Monotheistic religions in the beginning, called all people that were observing a Polytheistic religions—Pagans. That also called them idolaters, nonbelievers or gentile—but it did not stop them to absorb their holidays. Especially Christianity—which matched almost all of their holidays to Pagan's days of celebration. It was probably easier to convert people that way. Also, remember all of the ancient stories—which I wrote in the Book on Life, like the Story of Gilgamesh, with a "big flood" story—doesn't it sound like a Monotheistic flood story? There were some big floods before of course, but none had covered whole Earth; early humans were just believing it did—because it looked like to them that it did. How would "ark believers" explain—Kangaroos leaving the arc, and making it all the way to Australia, without leaving any bones behind—just as one simple example. And a lot of other stories, like ethical maxim: "Do not do to others what you do not want done to yourself," which I said—that it was coined by Confucius. How about "eye for eye" story? I am sure, you understand what I mean.

27.

It was not, till probably around the fifth century of Common Era—that the church officially decided for December 25^(th) as the birthday of the good man Jesus. It is well known, that Jesus was not born on that day—instead it is believed that it is the day of celebration for the Pagan's sun God—which was observed near the winter solstice. Many scholars believe—that the early Christians had chosen that date of this celebration—to interest more Pagans into Christianity. A similar thing is believed for Christian's most important holiday, Easter, where Christians celebrate Jesus Christ's resurrection from the dead. It is closely connected—to the Jewish holiday Passover. As a matter of fact, in the Greek or Spanish language, Easter is actually called the same name as Passover. Before this holiday was adopted into Christianity in Northern Europe—Pagan's celebrated Eostre, which was the Teutonic goddess of spring and fertility, at the same time of the year. Because of the similarity of the name, and time of the year it comes, it is widely believed that the old German word Eostre became—Easter; and that the Pagan holiday became part of the Christianity. Christmas trees, and reindeers, were part of the Pagan tradition too. Growing up in former Yugoslavia all of the kids, regardless of their religion, loved Santa Clause—whose name literary translates to Grandpa Frost—and me included. The only difference is most of us did not connect him to Christianity, I grew up believing, that he brings presents for the New Year—not Christmas. Regardless, from where holidays came to existence from, they are great. Holidays connect people, and for a moment almost everyone forgets all of the small troubles they have. Any kind of celebration, religious or personal, makes people happy. Especially for the kids, who get very happy for the holidays—they get toys, or money—which by the way started fairly recently. Now-days most kids get very nice gifts—but what I have heard, even till the twentieth century gifts were symbolic, like a small wooden toy, or a piece of candy. If you ask me, three holidays per year should be pretty enough—for all people on this Earth. That should be everyone's birthday, a two-day New Year's Eve and Day celebration, as one holiday—and July first, including the eve before—celebrating half of the year, that we had to achieve something—as another holiday. All three should be spent in appreciation of the Supreme Energy—which should be called Dear God, and of course there should be a lot of presents for everyone—but who am I to suggest? So, keep on celebrating whatever you like—hey it is a free world, and you decide what you want to believe in.

28.

When sports teams play good, that is because there is harmony in between the teammates—but when it is time for the team to sell the player, everyone looks at his individual worth. Same thing goes for life, we have to live in harmony with the world, be nice to everything in nature, and people too. When we die we will be judged individually—by how we were behaving in this world; not as member of a group of people in certain culture, or part of any religion—but as an individual. If you are a good person, who left a nice legacy behind—there is nothing you should be worrying, in the case you die. The bottom line is, it does not really pay to be bad and evil, it will definitely not have a good outcome—fight with the bad spirits around you, and everything will be fine. Good spirits were good people. Be strong, and be good, please.

BOOK ON WEALTH

1.

Profusion of any valuable source is wealth. Thanks to the accumulation
of wealth humans started using numbers—which also later grew to
the introduction of writing. As I wrote in the first part of this book,
hominins started collecting wealth—and they needed to keep
count of what they owned—thus, they started making marks on
wood, or stone. I am sure—that those valuable possessions brought
them a certain higher social status. Many times, archeologists have
discovered graves, that are a few thousand years old; and archeologists
can tell what social status that certain person, buried in that grave, had
belonged to, according to the wealth—which was buried with them.
Even today, wealthy people spend a lot of money for the funeral of the
loved one, it has not changed too much in the last few thousands of
years—wealth is wealth. However, being rich does not mean that they
have discovered what the meaning of life is. Their affluent status in
society can bring them a lavish life, but again they are mortal, same
as all people are. The main question is, if they used their material
wealth to leave any legacy behind, or not. If they did, their wealth
was used properly. Just being rich does not buy you a higher status in
the afterlife—but if you are smart enough, it can definitely help you.
Being mentally wealthy, is actually more important, then having all
of the material possessions. Having all of the material wealth, without

intellectual wealth, is like owning a Ferrari—but not knowing how to drive it.

2.

Since I came to America—I was always fascinated with the Smithsonian Institution. It is a museum, and a research complex—which includes nineteen museums and galleries. It also includes the National Zoological Park, as well as, different research facilities. For many years I have subscribed to the Smithsonian magazine, and every time I would receive a copy of the magazine in the mail, I get excited like a little kid getting candy. If a certain thing is named after somebody—or if some place bears the name of somebody, usually that person has discovered it, built it, left a huge personal legacy, or donated their wealth—so it was named after them for the sake of respect. In 1826, a wealthy British scientist, James Smithson left his will, where he named his nephew as beneficiary. In addition, he also wrote that if his nephew dies without any heirs, he wanted his money to go "to found at Washington, under the name of the Smithsonian Institution, an establishment for the increase and diffusion of knowledge among men," even though—he had no connections to the United States of America. According to the Smithsonian Institution, Mr. Smithson's nephew died suddenly at a young age, without having any heirs—six years after Mr. Smithson died. U.S. President Andrew Jackson announced Mr. Smithson bequest to the Congress—which accepted the legacy bequeathed to the nation, and pledged the faith of the United States to the charitable trust on July 1, 1836. Remains of Mr. Smithson were transported in 1903, from Genoa in Italy, where he was originally buried—to the Castle inside the Smithsonian Institution. The great American inventor Alexander Graham Bell personally escorted remains from Italy. When things are donated properly—it shows that it can create a huge legacy. Mr. Smithson's donation had such a significant impact on the arts, humanities, and sciences in the

United States—and the whole world. The slogan on the Smithsonian Institution web site says: "Seriously Amazing," which honestly they really are.

3.

I am sure, that there are not too many people in the world that have not heard of Microsoft, or Bill Gates. According to Mr. Gates' official blog web-site he is a technologist, business leader, and philanthropist. For most people a College education is crucial for success in life—but in the case of Bill Gates it was not necessary. As a young adult he had envisioned "a computer on every desktop and in every home," together with his friend Paul Allen, and in 1975 they had started, now the iconic—company Microsoft. Luckily for the whole world, their vision became reality, in many parts of the world. Thanks to them, and also to another amazing individual, and their competitor Steve Jobs—personal technology became an integral part of society today. Allen and Gates have left their leading position at Microsoft, after they had put it on the right track; and since then they have dedicated their life to philanthropy—for the most part. Mr. Gates says that he is passionate about Microsoft's work, and will always be involved with the company; including his present role as a member of the board, and technology advisor. In my opinion, if anyone in the world knows what the purpose of the one's life is—that would be Bill Gates. Forbes Magazine got me into following his life closely in the last fifteen years—and I have to admit, that in the beginning I did not have too positive of an opinion; maybe I was too young and inexperienced, thus I was thinking Bill Gates is just a lucky geek—who has a lot of money. Actually, the story would probably end like that, if he did not dedicate his life to the good life—and married a wonderful and smart wife. If he was changing "trophy wives" like socks, and if he was burning his wealth in heretical manner—I am sure, I would not mention him in this book as a role model. People can change—I hope that he does not. As of now, he is a living legend.

4.

Actually, marrying Melinda (née French) is one of the best things Bill Gates ever did, in my opinion. It looks to me that they live a proper life—and the combination of the two of them is bringing good to the world. In the year 2000, they had started the Bill and Melinda Gates Foundation, which is controlled by tree trustees—them and another amazing individual—Warren Buffet—who is, by the way, one of the most successful investors—that ever lived on Earth, if not the best. Bill and Melinda were raised properly, and have inherited the tradition of giving. On Bill and Melinda Gates' Foundation website it says: "Both the Gates and French families instilled the values of volunteerism and civic engagement. Our families believed that if life happens to bless you, you should use those gifts as well and as wisely as you can." This is it, the life worth living. They are not like some selfish people, who never realize—that the more you give—the more you get back. Simple as that, proverb "what goes around comes around" is in the full effect, again. In an attempt to make this book not too long I will mention just a couple of things this foundation did. In 2002, their foundation completed efforts to help install 47,000 computers in 11,000 libraries, in all 50 states—and in 2013, Bill helped launch a $5.5 billion effort to eradicate polio—an infectious disease caused by the poliovirus which causes paralysis, by the year 2018. Gates' family deeply holds on to the belief, that all lives have an equal value, and that's the key. Good people value life of any race or color. Just look at this, Confucius was Chinese, da Vinci was Italian, Gandhi was Indian, Mandela was black African, Lincoln was white American—but who cares about their skin color, culture, or nationality; we remember them as great people, role models of the life worth living. Whoever thinks that lives don't have an equal value, is not a good person.

Another thing that I admire, is that their foundation is focused in the areas of the health and education all around the world—which is the base for the good life, the life that is lived according to the moral rules, and doing of the right things.

5.

There is nothing wrong with enjoying life. If you worked hard, and made a lot of wealth—you deserve to live good, luxury kind of life— but of course luxury life without going into extremism. As I said before, with my job I have transported many wealthy individuals—and I have developed the gift of recognizing people that made their wealth on their own, from the ones that have inherited it. Many drivers, including me, use Google website to learn more about our customers—to know who we are picking up. If I had forgotten to "Google" my customer ahead of the pick-up; and it turned out somebody was nasty and rude, I would "Google" them after the pick-up—just to verify if I was right. By my experience, people that made their wealth are very friendly, down to earth, happy, and respectful—and those that are rude and disrespectful are usually the ones that inherited their wealth. I drove quite a few of those—and those are the ones who think they are in the center of the Universe. They also think, that everyone should be honored to serve them. Most people that inherited the wealth— don't have appreciation for money, and mostly take everything for granted—because they did not have to work for anything. They don't understand that we are all equal, from taxi drivers to them—all the same. We all breathe the same air, go to the restroom, sleep, absolutely the same. We are also equal—because we will all die too, no wealth can help them beat that. What many of them don't know, is what legacy one leaves behind—is the key; but you have to work for it yourself, only yourself.

6.

Just a few days ago, in the news, I had read that Mr. A.P.J. Abdul Kalam had died. He was a scientist, who turned out to be a good politician, and President of India from 2002 to 2007. In between many smart and good things he said during his life—I personally like this one the most: "Look at the sky. We are not alone. The whole universe is friendly to us and conspires only to give the best to those who dream and work." It's all said right there; all you need is to imagine it and work for it, I would also add to it—don't expect to get things for free. It is always better to make your wealth—then to inherit it. Many wealthy people had signed "The Giving Pledge," the campaign's website says that it "is an effort to invite the wealthiest individuals and families in the world to commit to giving the majority of their wealth to philanthropy." It was started by Warren Buffet, along with Bill and Melinda Gates—and I think it is a great idea. The pledge campaign— is not to sign legal contract with donations—it is more like a moral commitment. Buffet and Gates know it's a free world after all, every person or family that donate the wealth, is doing that for their own good. I follow the list all the time, and I am very glad when I see a new name added to the Pledge. When I saw Elon Musk, and Mark Zuckerberg joined the list, I was very happy—I always had a feeling they were good people. For the last twenty five years, there is TED (Technology, Entertainment, Design) conference, every single year. Their slogan is "Ideas Worth Spreading," and over the years they had many famous speakers spreading their ideas. Last year in 2014, Bill and Melinda Gates were speaking to the conference organizer—and they said—that they had prepared their three kids—not to inherit billions from them. Ms. Melinda said: "...they so know that our family belief is about responsibility..," and Mr. Bill said: "...they need to have a sense that their own work is meaningful and important..." This is what all wealthy parents should do—give your children some money, good healthcare coverage, and the best education. The children have to make their own legacy.

7.

I do not want you to think that this whole Wealth section of the book is dedicated just to Gates—so, even though I could mention many more things about them, like saving lives around the world—I will now go on with the book—but I have to mention one more good thing about them, that their marriage seems to be combination of honesty and trust. Marriage is a tremendous wealth. For example, I love my family more than words can express, and even this book would have not been written, if I did not have my wonderful family. As a matter of fact, I asked my friends and customers, what they think is the most important thing they did during their life? I asked them that question just out of curiosity—and did not mention that it is for a book. Almost all have said: "My family," thinking of their spouse, and their children. As for the same reason, I asked some of them: What is their legacy in the world? Most have answered again: "Well, my kids are my everything, and that is what I am leaving behind." Well, I agree to a certain point, but I strongly believe—that the parents and the kids have to leave separate good legacies. Regardless, the institution of marriage is very important for a healthy mind, and a reason to build the wealth. Having a family pushes us to work harder, and think of life more—and value life more in general. In my case, I always worked very hard—as I said before—I worked many weeks between sixty, and a hundred hours per week, without a day off. Every day, I shaved and had put a tie on—and I had sometimes, over 250 days working straight, seven days per week, without a day off. At the moment, these days, I am mostly home, writing this book, and it feels like a long vacation; but I will come back to that hard work, as soon as I finish writing this book, because we live on the credit cards now— and I will pay them all off, as soon as possible—when I start working full-time again. What is my motif? The answer is my family. I want my children to know what I think about life, and to teach them—that hard work is important. Also, I have a pledge to my wife, that I will pay all the bills on time, and I have no doubts that I will definitely do it. We went through a similar financial situation a few years ago, and that experience made me stronger—much stronger.

8.

In 2008, and 2009, my business was very slow; and my wife being a teacher's assistant was not making a lot of money either—so our family had a hard time keeping up with all the bills that were coming. I talked to her about if we should miss our mortgage payment on our house, and I gave her all different examples of my colleagues, that are not paying their house for months, and they were still not losing their house. That was where she showed me her strong character; her answer was, "No way, if we cannot pay the mortgage we are leaving from this house tomorrow, we have signed the contract, and we made a commitment—which we have to fulfill," the next morning I wrote one of the credit card's blank checks to my name, and deposited it to the bank, so we could send the mortgage payment. I had to do it again—on two more occasions later. Many people would call that—financial suicide, but in my case it saved me my house. Those years I had accumulated a lot of debt—but I have never ever missed a payment on anything, from my house mortgage to my cars' payments, insurance or credit cards. With my hard work, by 2012 I was pretty much debt free—except for the house mortgage, which is on 30 years. We still live in the same house, which we might have lost if I did not have such a strong answer from my wife. So, credit cards are very helpful if you have the intent to return the money—but it has to be on-time. People that have trouble with credit cards are those who miss their on-time payments—or don't have serious intent to return the money, that is where credit cards get you, those companies can be brutal with the fees—but if you pay it all on-time—it's all good. An absurd of our society is, when I asked one financial adviser who is a friend of mine, how to lower my house payment—he told me: "Honestly, you have to miss a couple of payments on the mortgage, and that is the only way the bank will work with you on lowering your mortgage payment," he continued: "The government will help only if you are behind on your mortgage payments." It means people get awarded if they miss a payment on their house mortgage, and if you pay your mortgage on-time—you get no help, nonsense—but true. This was my own life experience, and as I said above—it made me much stronger.

9.

Marriage is a contract too, like any other contract. If spouses stand together, honor the marriage contract, and fight against troubles together—they will win in the end. The divorce rate around the world is so high, because people don't take that paper, which they have signed, seriously. People are stubborn—and don't want to agree on how to solve some issues. Sometimes, one side has to let it go, and accept the other side's suggestion. If you talk to your spouse openly—most problems could be solved. I support marriage, where people stay together, and help each other all the time—but there are some people, that have an open marriage, and both partners agree to allow each other to have relationships with other people—in the same time. The most famous example of that marriage was in the case of the legendary musician—Bob Marley. He left an extraordinary legacy behind him—even though he smoked cannabis, and had a very open marriage with his wife—Rita Anderson. He was still a good man, because he did not hide anything from his wife. They agreed on that, and had kids together, but they both also had kids with other partners—while still being married. It sounds very complex, but they made it work just fine. Both were open to each other, respected each other life's decisions—and had a deep understanding of each other.

Bob respected Rita, and rightfully he left her to inherit most of his wealth, after he died. It was of course not a marriage type I support, but they had made it work. As long as they had an agreement in-between themselves, then is was alright. The only time when one spouse can get forgiveness for cheating is if the other spouse approved it—every other attempt without approval is assault to the marriage contract. In 1999, Time magazine named Bob Marley's music album Exodus, the best album of the 20ᵗʰ century. I like Bob Marley and Jamaican people in general. I have a few friends from Jamaica—and they are all happy, friendly, and respectful. You have to be sincere to your spouse, and to the whole world also. People can feel things, wrong or good doings cannot be hidden. If people are not honest to each other, then sooner or later it comes out, and usually it comes out in the form of Murphy's law, when "Anything that can go wrong, will go wrong," that also applies for anything in the life—including marriage of course. Do the right thing, be honest, be sincere, talk to your spouse and understand each other. Save the marriage. Don't do things behind spouses back, don't hurt anybody, because as I said before—all that we are doing is recorded—and if it does not come to daylight in this life, it will lower your points in the afterlife—for sure. It is in your cloud of earthly doings, it has a life of its own—which cannot be erased, but can be fixed, while there is still time. Be honest, and everything will be alright.

10.

During my hard financial times in 2008, I had showed one weakness—which many other people have. I was hoping, every day—to win the lottery. I was able to keep it under control, and did not play more than $10 per week; but my mind was blurred—it was constantly on my mind. Stopping at the gas stations, almost every day, was part of my job—and that is where I was buying the most lottery tickets. It was very sad to see some people buying a paycheck worth of lottery tickets, right in front of me—and next drowning nobody would win the jack pot, I have felt bad for them. In the same time they taught me a lesson: $10 or $500 really does not matter really much—if you are supposed to win—you will win. Around the same time I had read in the news, that one old lady here in Florida, had won millions on the lottery—with just one ticket purchased. So, since 2008, I play one ticket only, and it is just once in a while—not all the time. I have no idea how it works, but like idiom "watched phone never rings," when you hope for something to happen—usually it does not—but when you give up the worrying, things start getting better. Having self-control is the most important for anything. I do believe, that by our thinking we can make an influence on things—but we cannot make it happen. Anyway, in the same time I looked at other ways on how to make money, and was thinking about the Law of attraction—which totally contradicts that "watched phone" theory. I have already read a few books on the subject, and in between the books that I own at home, I've found: The science of getting rich, book written in 1910, by Wallace D. Wattle—that interested me. I am not too sure how I had gotten that book at all—but I am glad that I have it in my collection. Interesting enough, in the same period of time, book The Secret by Rhonda Byrne, got my attention at the airport book store, while I was waiting to pick somebody up. Without even knowing, that those books were connected, I had purchased it.

11.

I find it amazing how things sometimes work out. It is possible, that when we start thinking about something, somehow things connected to it enter your life. If we think about somebody, it is possible, that soon we will meet them somewhere, unplanned—or receive a call from them. Many people would say that is telepathy; I like the idea, but there is no scientific evidence that telepathy is a real phenomenon. I think the answer is—that Energy, in that cloud, that follows us all the time. We cannot make things happen, or make somebody do certain things with our thinking—but can leave idea in the Ether. The cloud has everything, from our ideas to our thoughts, and records of all our doings. I am convinced that Energy in the air exists, and it is synchronized to all the things we do or think of—again we cannot make an influence on it, we just give it a life. Many books have been written about the Law of attraction idea, and they all pretty much claim that it works—some almost say guaranteed. I came up with the conclusion that the Law of attraction works to a certain point. I definitely don't think, that just by being concentrated on a certain wish—that wish will come true. We can give the wish a life, and then it depends on many factors—if we will be strong enough to bring it to reality. It is not only us, it is also chemical. That cloud, that follows us everywhere, is a chemical substance of gas that is composed of a particular set of molecules or ions—that are not visible to humans. The secret is that different people have different strengths to absorb energy, as I explained in the religion part of this book—so it may work for some—but it may not for others. Some people are stronger, and some weaker, physically and mentally. Hence, the Law of attraction works on some, and it does not work for other individuals. Be strong!

12.

As I have mentioned a few times in this book, we are all connected, not just people, but the whole Universe—again that is for the reason—that we are all made up of the same matter. Also the idea of Ether, where I said I believe those invisible personal clouds exist—can have an influence on different things. I find it very interesting; that some of the biggest popular discoveries in different fields, have been discovered around the same time—independently. Many times, people that discovered something of the same nature, did it at about the same time—even though, they lived in a whole different area, and had no physical connection. For example, the mathematical study of change called Calculus, was discovered in the 17th century, by the great physicist Sir Isaac Newton in England, and also by the great polymath and philosopher Gottfried Wilhelm von Leibniz in Germany—independently, or use of Telegraph was discovered independently same year, in 1837, by Charles Wheatstone in England, and Samuel Morse in America. Even more striking is that Elisha Gray and Alexander Bell filed for the patent on the Telephone—on the same day, in 1876, or how about the discovery of radioactivity, that was done independently by Silvanus Thompson and Henri Becquerel, in 1896. As I said before—when you get the idea you also give it a life. Once your idea is in the Ether, and somebody who is mentally strong, can absorb the energy—can get the same idea, which looks like, and for discoverers is—independent. You can obtain wealth, and fame, by knowing how to penetrate in to many great ideas in the Ether. That knowledge is very useful, and only few are naturally capable of achieving it—but many others can achieve it by training their mind. By deep concentration, you can find the answer to a lot of things— because answers already exist somewhere in the Ether. You are not stealing the ideas—you are actually understanding the ideas. Believe me, the answer to anything is "in the air".

13.

People also create different energies, positive or negative, about certain things in life. If some movie or book became popular, it gets criticized by the masses. More positive, and honest approach can boost ratings of particular movie or certain book, and can even get it to a higher position—then what it is really worth. For that reason, it is good to be honest; and do things right—because people can feel it. I also find it interesting—that when people like a certain celebrity, that celebrity person can get into a higher respect area, then their real value is. But if that same individual does something wrong, or unethical, that same mass of people will create negative energy towards that celebrity person—which will possibly leave that celebrity person in pain. Everyone, especially celebrities, should show gratitude to the Universal energy for things they have achieved. Gratitude was best explained by the German philosopher and theologian Meister Eckhart, when he said: "If the only prayer you said was thank you that would be enough." We all have to appreciate the things we have—but it is in a human nature to take things for granted. When I meet people at the airport, and let's say the weather is bad, their immediate reaction is: "Hey you are supposed to have nice weather here in Florida—all the time." When we get some bad weather here, then we learn to appreciate the nice sunny days, which we have in Florida, most of the time—and we should appreciate it. That applies to everything—and every day, we should say: Thank You Dear God—for everything.

14.

The Universe feels our attitude, and the more we are thankful the more we will get in return. Nobody has to know about it—you can show gratitude quietly, just say it inside yourself: Thank You Universe. As I said, it's all recorded in the cloud—so all you need to do, as a matter of fact—is to think of thankfulness. Thank the Universe, and the Universe will award you with even more. That is another way to accumulate wealth. If the owner of a company shows respect and gratitude to the employees, he will get the same in return—possibly even more. People that show gratitude, are naturally more happy and social; they make easy contacts, because if we show appreciation to somebody—chances are very huge, that we will get appreciation in return. The great Roman philosopher, and statesman—Markus T. Cicero has said: "Gratitude is not only the greatest of virtues, but the parent of all others." And again, it has to be sincere, deep from the heart, as Mother Theresa once said: "It's not how much we give, but how much love we put into giving," and listen to the one of the most influential lady's in the world—Oprah Winfrey. She has a huge life experience; and listen when she says: "Be thankful for what you have; you'll end up having more. If you concentrate on what you don't have, you will never, ever have enough." You have to acknowledge the benefit, if you have learned or earned something, show gratitude, that's all.

15.

There are many factors that can make the influence, and it will make a difference in obtaining wealth, and legacy. Except from how strong your mind is to absorb the ideas from the Universe—hard work is the key. Our mind could be strong—and we can be talented at something, but without hard work, we still will not obtain our full potential. Many times, the story of Drazen Petrovic comes to my mind. He grew up not too far from the place where Nikola Tesla grew up. As a basketball player he had left a huge legacy. Before he died, in a car accident at the age of 28, Drazen had won many medals, from the Olympic Games to FIBA World Cup and FIBA EuroBasket medals too. By many, he was considered the best basketball shouting guard ever, and after he died he was introduced to both, NBA and FIBA, Basketball Hall of Fame. Except fame and legacy his professional basketball contracts brought him millions of dollars—and he had deserved that wealth. As a young kid he used to shoot the ball at the basket for a few hours per day, every single day. In the ESPN's 30 for 30: Once Brothers TV series, Drazen's mom said: "He had the keys to the gym, and he would wake up at 6am" to practice. He had a lot of talent of course— but without hard work, he definitely would not have succeeded this much. In the book named Drazen Petrovic, by Mario Zovko, it was written that Drazen said: "For me this (hard work) was perfectly normal. If by some reason I didn't go to practice, and this could only be purely co-incidental, I would immediately get sick. For me to miss practice was almost like a deadly sin." Regardless of how talented we are, with hard work we can, and will, succeed much more. Everyone is trying to reach the "American Dream," all around the world—it became sort off international slogan for the better life. I personally have heard people in Europe call it "American Dream," when they achieved something great. It is the same dream for the young guy, or gal, in Japan or America, Europe or India, or anywhere else in the world—it's the absolutely the same dream. We all want to find a good job, many people dream of spouses and kids, and definitely all dream about how to build a lot of wealth. Wealth is "American Dream"—Wealth is the Universal dream. It is in our hands, we have to dream of achieving big things, work hard, be honest, show respect and gratitude—and it can happen.

BOOK ON HEALTH

1.

It is customary—that people all around the world, when congratulating someone's birthday, wish that person a lot of wealth, and of course—good health. That is the most common toast for hundreds of years—and will be in the future. Health is an essential part of living the good life. Once you are healthy—everything else is not as important. When we get sick, that is when we start to appreciate, and realize, that having good health is all that we need. Many times, terminally ill patients wished, that they had lived a healthier life, had eaten healthier, and had worked less. The common thing to most humans, regardless of the area of the world where they live, is that in a material world people sacrifice their health—to obtain material possessions. I am sure that many wealthy individuals would trade all the wealth they own, for good health—in the case they would get terminally ill, just to be healthy. Even though, there are still some people in the world, which don't appreciate the good health that they already have. I have heard, which might have been a joke that people in some places are trying to sell their own kidney, just to buy the latest technology gadgets. What if that joke is true? Would it really be worth it to damage your health, just to buy a new technology thing—which will be absurd in the next five years? Of course not.

2.

Health is the most important, with good health, we can enjoy life, start a family, and go to work. Still, we should not work over the limit—the limit which our body can take. I have learned hard way, that working too hard is not good for the health; four years ago I had fallen down to the floor, while waiting for somebody, at the airport. I had recognized the message my body had sent me, a little too-late—but still on-time; and I definitely think, that was a wakeup call for me. Even though, I had lost consciousness just for a second—I had still ended up hitting my head on the floor, which luckily was a carpet. After that—I've learned when I need to stop. We all have to realize that our body has a limit of what it can handle, which varies from person to person. A few times after that experience, when I had felt that something was not right with my body—I had stopped working, and went home. Even this break from work, to write this book, is planned also to rejuvenate my health. I remember, when I came back home that day, I decided to write this book, even more, as soon as possible—it was on my mind for a few hours. My health was affected by my hard work, and I was diagnosed with high blood pressure—at my age of 36. There are many life lessons out there, for everyone, we just need to recognize them. I have learned my lesson. Well, at least I think I have.

3.

There are many factors that can damage good health. Except hard work and not eating properly, stress is probably at the top of the list. When we are young and go to school, we have our first experience with stress—all the homework, and worrying about tests we have to take—but that is like a child's game, compared to all the stress we have when we grow up. Naturally, human beings worry about many things. We as adults, always worry about job security, debt and financial security, love, kids, parents, and health. Some people even worry about getting old. The more we worry, the more of a hormone called Cortisol our body produces. That hormone is popularly called—stress hormone. I had heard about that hormone about ten years ago, when stress started affecting me. At that time we had moved to a different city— purchased a house and new furniture, I'd changed the company, and turned 30 years old—too many things were happening at the same time. Till then, I really did not feel much stress, except my school time, and the time I had spent in the war zone. I did not have any student's loans, and I did not own any property—till then. It seemed to me—that with the increase of the wealth—there was an increase of the stress. Maybe that's why religious monks, which don't own anything—are pretty much stress free.

4.

Then, looking deeper to learn about Cortisol, I had found on about. com, a beautifully written article by Elizabeth Scott—who is a stress management expert. In a few words I had learned that, Cortisol is involved in our body's metabolism, body's immune function, regulation of blood pressure, insulin release for blood sugar maintenance, inflammatory response etc. With the more stress our body produces the more Cortisol, and prolonged time with high Cortisol level in the body, will course blood sugar imbalance, will decrease bone density and muscle tissue. It will also cause higher blood pressure, and will lower our body's immunity and inflammatory responses—it will slow the healing of any wounds, and other health consequences. Living a stress free life, will definitely also mean—living a healthier life. Even on a regular basis when somebody upsets us at work, or even driving in traffic, it will make our body produce more Cortisol. Try not to worry about things you cannot change, with that worrying you just waist your energy for nothing; as the popular old proverb in the Balkan area says: "You cannot steer the curvy river Drina." Don't forget, stress will damage your body, and once your body gets weaker—it opens the possibility for cancer to form, and grow. Living a healthy life, with physical exercise every day—will possibly dramatically reduce the production of the stress hormones.

5.

A healthy life style will set the foundation for leaving a legacy. When our health is good, we can concentrate on building something that will last—but when our health is bad, we will most likely concentrate only on trying to improve our health. In some cases damaged health, injury, illness, paralyses, missing body parts, blindness or other difficulties have inspired those affected people to try even harder, to do extra good things—and leave a legacy behind them. They are a special kind of people—because they try double as hard, then ordinary people. They are my heroes. The general condition of your body and mind combined usually has to be good to live a good life, but is not totally necessary, it only makes it much easier. Some of those special people, double hard workers as I said, are doing a great job in leaving a memorable legacy. The great Stephen Hawking is a theoretical physicist, and just thinking of him, amazes me. In his early twenties he was diagnosed with motor neuron disease, or Lou Gehrig's disease, which is the slow progressing form of amyotrophic lateral sclerosis—popularly called ALS. The disease did not stop him from leaving a remarkable legacy, and when his muscles started losing power—he always had found a way to still work hard. His book A Brief History of Time, which I am sure everybody has heard about, was published when he was 46 years old. That book had me interested in the cosmology, and the dynamics of the Universe in the 1990's—and I keep it in my books collection—as a special book. People diagnosed with the ALS live two to five years after being diagnosed—in most cases, but luckily Mr. Hawkins with his strong mind has beaten all the odds; and is living over fifty years with it. Not just living, but constantly working on new projects. He has also received over twenty notable rewards; and he should be an inspiration to all of us.

6.

With many theme parks, Orlando attracts millions of tourists every year—according to Wikipedia over fifty million in total. Many people also come to Orlando for different business conferences and conventions. It is one of the best place in the whole world, to have company meetings. Conventioneers feel safe to bring their families with them, ultimately combining business and pleasure. I have realized, when people come here for the meetings, they are usually the most excited to learn—who the guest speaker for their meeting will be. Most of the times—the guest speaker is a person who has a lot of experience in the field of business—that certain company is involved in; but sometimes they also have celebrities or inspirational speakers too. Every time, when I hear that a certain company will have an inspirational speaker, I am very excited to hear who it is going to be—and sometimes I get lucky enough to transport them. They are not inspirational speakers without a reason, of course, they all have interesting life stories to tell. Out of many speakers, which I have driven, one person amazed me the most—Jim Abbott. Honestly, I never followed baseball much, but Google helped me to get to know— who I was picking up. From our first contact at the airport I had felt a lot of positive energy from this person. His story is remarkable, it is outstanding. Mr. Abbott was born in 1967—without a right hand, but it did not stop him to fulfill his life's meaning. His parents encouraged him to play sports, and he was pretty good at a few. It turned out, that he was exceptionally good at baseball—and despite being born without a right hand he had made an amazing professional baseball career. When he was attending the University of Michigan in 1987, he had won the James E. Sullivan Award, which is given to the top amateur athlete in the United States. For his contribution to College sports, he was later elected into the College Baseball Hall of Fame. The following year in 1988, he had won a gold Olympic medal in Seoul, Korea—and have signed a professional baseball contract with the California Angels. While playing professionally, for ten years, with different teams—the most notable was, while pitching for the New York Yankees in 1993, he had pitched a no-hitter, against the Cleveland Indians. Post retiring, Mr. Abbott is doing a great job giving inspirational speeches—about his amazing life—of course. This is an example of life filled with constant double hard work. His book Imperfect: An Improbable Life, also has a special place on my bookshelf now.

7.

With these two unconnected individual stories, I want to show you—that Life is a Challenge, more for some—less for others. Even with all different obstacles, people can leave astonishing legacies behind. If people with disabilities have to use, double hard work, it means that if we are healthy and without issues, we should definitely learn from them. The only way to succeed is to try—and it has to be the best try—not a mediocre try. We must have those extraordinary people on our mind as inspiration. Nothing comes easy and on its own, we have to fight hard; and try to be as good as possible, period. The final conclusion is, that if we push even harder—we can reach even farther, then what we would normally reach. Remember Drazen Petrovic's story, he was healthy—and he pushed above what would be his regular best—by practicing basketball every day starting at 6am, and staying at the practice field extra time—he had developed into the best basketball player in Europe—and one of the best in the world. How about Nick Vujicic, he was born without both arms and both legs—which is known as tetra-amelia syndrome, in 1982. It is hard to imagine doing any regular tasks in life without having even one limb—but not having all four and finishing college at the age of

21—is simply extraordinary. As a young man, Nick did not give up positive thinking, and he has pretty much accomplished his purpose in life—as long as he continues doing a great job inspiring others, without doing anything illegal or unmoral. I have a deep feeling, that he is a very good man, and he will be alright. I might not agree with his evangelical Christian job, but I love him for being a good hardworking man—and an inspiration for people in the whole world—regardless of his religion. Just think again, without any limbs he had finished University at the age of 21, and now is happily married with two children, that's not just double work—that's astonishing! Thus far, he was an inspirational speaker to over three million people live in person, and many more over different media outlets. On his website attitudeisaltitude.com he wrote: "Dream big my friend and never give up. We all make mistakes, but none of us are mistakes. Take one day at a time. Embrace the positive attitudes, perspectives, principles and truths I share, and you too will overcome."

8.

Many of the people in the world are healthy, and strong—but waste their energy for nothing. They don't think about what their purpose in life is, and it turns out, that they just live like the plants—like a trees. Actually, some trees do even better than them, if they become a piano or violin. That average human just waits—for when it is their time to die—they kind of live life by going to work and paying bills—but that is it; no legacy-no life. It was a wasted life! They of course die unknown, and in the history of time, they will be forgotten quickly— as nobody will have a reason for remembering them, except their closest family members, for one generation. If we are healthy or able— we must leave a legacy. Be good to your health; because with good health it is much easier to create something. Many people take their health for granted, and don't take care of it. In my opinion, the number one reason for damaging our health is probably eating unhealthy, and second is abusing our own health by the use of drugs, legal and illegal. On a few websites, it was credited to the wonderful 14th Dalai Lama after he was asked the question what surprises him the most about humanity that he answered: "Man... sacrifice's his health in order to make money. Then he sacrifices money to recuperate his health. And then he is so anxious about the future that he does not enjoy the present; the result being that he does not live in the present or the future; he lives as if he is never going to die, and then dies having never really lived." Most likely, it was not said by the good man Dalai Lama, but James Lachard—and was published, as a part of the book called Interview with God, by Reata Strickland—she was probably unsure who originally wrote it, and signed it as Anonymous—which is fair. Regardless who wrote it, if you ask me—that is the best explanation of an average man's life. And by the way, listen to the 14th Dalai Lama a lot, because he has so many smart things to say—about everything. As we are all told by doctors, eating right and exercising is key to good health—but for many of us it takes a long time to understand that message. For some, that message is never understood.

9.

Otto Heinrich Warburg was one of the best 20th century's biochemists. In 1931, he had won the Nobel Prize in Physiology or Medicine, and he was nominated many more times, for the same award during his career. Except for being the Nobel laureate, he also was awarded the Iron Cross for bravery—during the First World War. On the official Nobel Prize website, it says that Mr. Warburg was awarded: "For his discovery of the nature and mode of action of the respiratory enzyme." At the Nobel-Laureates meeting on June 30th, 1966 Mr. Warburg gave a lecture—which English language edition was revised by Dean Burk of National Cancer Institute in USA—where it was said: "Cancer, above all other diseases, has countless secondary causes. But, even for cancer, there is only one prime cause. Summarized in a few words, the prime cause of cancer is the replacement of the respiration of oxygen in normal body cells by fermentation of sugar. All normal body cells meet their energy needs by respiration of oxygen, whereas cancer cells meet their energy needs in a great part by fermentation. All normal body cells are thus obligate aerobes....Oxygen gas, the donor of energy in plants and animals is dethroned in the cancer cells and replaced by an energy yielding reaction of the lowest living forms, namely, a fermentation of glucose." All those years have passed—and we still have not learned the lesson.

10.

I have to admit, that I am in love with the sugar too—even by writing this next paragraph—I have the feeling as if I am betraying my best friend. That is because I am addicted to it, most likely. It took me many years to realize—and start fighting with myself, not to intake too much sugar. As Mr. Warburg proved, sugar is the one to blame for the most part for cancer, as he explained—that healthy cells will become cancerous if oxygen is replaced by sugar—as cells deprived of oxygen will become cancerous. Sugar is helping the spread of cancer in the body too. You will be shocked to find out that sugar is more addictive—then heroin, for rodents, and possibly for humans too. Almost two years ago, I came over a great article on Forbes.com, written by Jacob Sullum; that mentioned a great study by Connecticut College students and a professor of psychology, about the influence of the sugar on lab rats. In this study, lab rats were exposed to the sugary foods—as well as the addictive drugs in the same space, amazingly enough—after some time rats in the lab started coming first to the sugary food instead of the drugs. With help from the students, neuroscientist Joseph Schroeder had concluded and said: "Our research supports the theory that high-fat/high-sugar foods stimulate the brain in the same way that drugs do,....It may explain why some people can't resist these foods despite the fact that they know they are bad for them." This great study also says: "The Oreo's activated significantly more neurons then cocaine or morphine." This Connecticut College study—and especially Mr. Warburg's work, should teach us, humans, about the negativity of sugar, in general. Even though, it looks like we are learning very slow—since it has been almost one hundred years from the time Mr. Warburg proved—that sugar in the form of glucose is causing and spreading cancer, I am convinced, that the world is not doing enough to educate people—not to consume too much sugar. I understand, that food, and pharmaceutical industries would lose billions of dollars, if sales of sugar dropped; but just think as a human being—that we have lost more people on this Earth to sugar, then to any wars combined.

11.

Here I have it. Life is giving me a lesson—right here—right now, live. Just after I had finished writing this paragraph on sugar I had stopped writing, and went to do my yearly, regular blood test. For the last couple of days—I don't know if I was trying to fool myself or the doctor—but I have been eating only soup. The reason for eating light, I think must be, because of last year test results, I ate a burger and fries that night before the test—so my blood test results came up with very disturbing numbers for me. This time I was trying to be smart—and I was trying to make my blood work numbers look good for this year—which is kind of foolish. Usually, I have my blood withdrawn in the lab quickly, and off to work I go. This time I came back home, planning to continue writing the next paragraph of this book. For the first hour back home, I was fine, then suddenly it had hit me. My own knees would not hold me, and I have laid down onto the floor, home alone. Most likely, the reason for my sudden body weakness, and that feeling like I will go unconscious, was because, I was only eating only that soup, for over fifty hours. My body probably became weak without any sugar in it. I'd gotten up slowly holding onto the furniture, and made it to the kitchen—where the first thing that I saw was a bag of pure granulated sugar. I took three big spoons of sugar itself, and poured it down my throat with water, the next thing I did was lay-down again. After a few minutes I started feeling better, thanks to Dear God—and the sugar, I guess.

12.

As life has it, my next paragraph was supposed to be about the terrible effects of carbonated sugary drinks, but instead of going back to continue writing against cola, I've gotten up and opened the refrigerator—and grabbed a can of cola—which I was very happy to see. It sounds very ironic, that a can of cola made me feel better—and a little bit later my strength started coming back. Regardless, I had to write this; not only that sugar-sweetened soft drinks can cause cancer, if used in large quantities, they will most likely cause obesity, dental caries—and possibly type 2 diabetes. Also, just a few days ago I'd watched a bunch of YouTube videos—about the dangerous side of cola. There are some videos that show you how you can clean rust off a metal bumper on a car, with use of cola and a rug only—or use cola as a chemical for cleaning many other things. Particularly, one video made me think about it, for the long time. That video was documented with a screenshot of an actual case number at the Court. A big company, producer of the sugary soda, had won the law suit over the guy—who claimed, that he had found a mouse in the can of their carbonated drink. The maker of the beverage claimed—that there was no way that the mouse would still be recognizable, because there was a whole month, since that can of soda was filled and sold. Maker of the soda claimed that the mouse would dissolve into the drink, leaving only a tail visible, in that period of time. Some YouTube guys tried the experiment, and proved that the beverage maker was right—and had rightfully won the law suit. Amazingly enough, and knowing that, I still occasionally drink some soda. You can Google the lawsuit story yourself, I am sure you will find it interesting.

13.

Many foods, and drinks being part of it, are dangerous for our health; but in small quantities they can be, as good as, medicine. Take alcohol for example, it has also probably killed more people than any wars combined, but it is almost unimaginable to live a modern human life—without it. Every hospital in the world must have some alcohol— as it kills a lot of bacteria, it has saved many lives too. In my life, I do not close the doors for anything—like some people would say: "I will never drink alcohol in my life," or "I will never drink soda again," but not me. Even though, I know that most carbonated drinks are very acidic, and loaded with sugar, and very dangerous for my health, I still appreciate the good side of soda. When I had opened that can of cola, after laying down—I had felt like it was the best medicine in the whole world. It definitely helped me get my strength back; but again knowing the bad side of it, I will try to cut the use of it as much as possible—but will not totally cut it. Same with alcohol, I do not drink it on a regular basis, but if I feel that it could be used as medicine—I will not swear that I will not use it. Again, it is our free will, and we decide for ourselves. Too much of anything is not good, and we know what is right and what is wrong, so we need to behave as intellectual humans. I agree with Hippocrates when he said: "Extreme remedies are very appropriate for extreme diseases."

14.

The worst thing is to do something bad, knowingly, and then try to blame it on something, or somebody else. I agree, that some things should be kept in hospitals only. For example heroin—as from a chemical standpoint, is very similar to morphine. Heroin, according to the U.S. National Library of Medicine, is made from natural morphine that is extracted from the certain poppy plant seeds. I cannot imagine a modern hospital without morphine, people would be in so much pain without it. But keep it there, in the hospitals only—where it belongs. Many dangerous chemicals are very good in small quantities, at the right places of use, problems happen—when people start abusing it. Only professionals know what the right amount is, because that is what they are trained for. Many deaths in the world are caused by legal, and illegal drug overdoses. According to Getsmartaboutdrugs.com—except death—overdose symptoms can cause slow and shallow breathing, convulses, clammy skin, blue lips and fingernails, and comas. People abusing drugs are putting their life at risk, in most cases, without leaving any legacy. Using drugs makes their life worthless. Even if they have left a legacy while alive—their death from drug overdose will definitely damage the legacy. As the old proverb goes: "If you play with the fire, eventually you will get burned," same goes for drugs; if you play with the drugs eventually you will suffer from them. Remember that.

15.

There is the possibility, that sometimes we heal ourselves just by thinking, and hoping, that certain thing will help us. Many times, the reason for not feeling good has a neurophysiological basis. Sometimes, it is all a product of our imagination. In psychiatry there is the term hypochondriac—which is the name for the people that worry about their health excessively. Those people usually focus on some symptoms of a certain illness, and start believing that is what they have. I believe, that earlier mentioned the Law of Attraction could be used for fighting hypochondria. If you convince yourself, deep inside your mind, that nothing is wrong with you—it possibly can trigger some neurons—which will actually make you start feeling better. A similar technique doctors use in some countries, for actual medical purposes. In their case it is called Placebo effect. Doctors would just give a patient something, such as sugar pills, and would tell that patient it will cure their illness. Amazingly enough—sometimes it works. After believing in that, and being sure it is the medicine, something gets triggered in the body, which somehow helps them—our body is powerful. The Great Hippocrates said: "A wise man should consider that health is the greatest of human blessings, and learn how by his own thought to derive benefit from his illnesses." Think about it. It has been all said before. There are cures for everything, the only thing we have to do is to study—to investigate. We have to be good to our health—because again, Health is essential!

BOOK ON DEATH

1.

The end of life is called death. When vital functions of living organisms cease to operate—then the termination of all biological functions begins. Death could occur by force—or by natural causes. Nobody has ever managed to live forever, within the human body. In my opinion, human dying, is connected only, to the soul leaving the body; as I have mentioned in the religion part of this book—I believe the soul continues to live, after death of the body, in the unseen area, which was explained by early philosophers—that area is called Ether. If you remember, I also mentioned, that most people who had a clinical death would explain after, that once they have temporarily died—they were able to see their actual body from outside—also they remembered everybody and everything—but they also, were not able to make any contact, to live human beings. My conclusion is, that the brain keeps information temporary—but the soul maybe even eternally. Knowing that one day we will unavoidably die, we should, as soon as possible, think of how we will be remembered.

2.

Ultimately, we need future generations of people of the world to remember us for something, good things we have done—or things we have created. Even if we don't get lucky enough to gain people's recognition on the world level, and if our work stays noticed just between our families—it is still a good legacy; it is still very important, that our friends and family remember us as a good person. Regardless, we have to give our best before we die—to at least try to give an important contribution—for the good of humankind, to leave a profound impact on the society; and time will tell, if our work was memorable. Remember, that many people that we celebrate today, were not recognized as very important people while they were alive. Many of them, even died in poverty. The interesting thing is, that they enjoyed their work regardless—and even without being recognized they still gave their best. The most important is, that they did not get discouraged. Today in America, we cannot imagine libraries, without having books by Edgar Allan Poe or Emily Dickinson—but while they were alive both of them were fairly unknown.

3.

If the great works, of Ms. Dickinson or Mr. Poe were recognized, at the time they were alive; the same way as their works are recognized now, perhaps they both would have been celebrities. I am positive, that there would have been a chance for them to live for a much longer time— then what they actually did; Mr. Poe died at the age of forty, and Ms. Dickinson at the age of fifty-five. Regardless, they still gave their best for the circumstances they were at, recognized or not. Even though, sometimes I wonder if they had lived longer, if there would be a huge possibility that we would have more interesting books, written by them. One of my all-time favorite authors—Mark Twain, was forty years old, when he wrote The Adventures of Tom Sawyer, and forty-nine years old when he wrote Adventures of Huckleberry Finn. Luckily, he was famous while he was alive. By the way, Dr. Seuss was fifty-four years old when he wrote The Cat in the Hat. How about our dear naturalist and geologist Charles Darwin, who showed us that we all have descended from a common ancestor; his work was explained in his book On the Origin of Species. He was fifty years old—when that book was published. It is hard to find anyone in the world that has not heard of polymath Leonardo Da Vinci. He was excellent in sculpting, science, painting, architecture, music, mathematics, writing, engineering, invention, cartography, etc. His legacy to humankind is definitely remarkable—as he is one of the most important individuals—that ever lived on Earth. Interestingly enough, most people will connect his name, to the single painting called—Mona Lisa. He was already about fifty-one years old, when he started painting the Mona Lisa. The bottom line is, that if we stay healthy, and hopefully have obtained financial security (which is not requirement, but will help), it's never too late to create a master-piece. We have to work hard on it, or for it, and time will tell if we did a good job.

4.

Talking about the "time will tell" idiom, as I already mentioned Nikola Tesla, and his smart prediction: "The present is theirs; the future, for which I really worked, is mine," there is also another great individual, whose work did not get recognized immediately—and that is Alfred Wegener. Thanks to him, we now know that very large landmasses on Earth, called continents, are drifting apart. Don't get me wrong, he was already fairly known as a good meteorologist, and as a pioneer of polar research; but his hypothesis about continental drift received big skepticism from geologists at that time. Maybe, for the reason— that Wegener was not an actual geologist, and for them he did not qualify for the work. It took many years, after he died, that his major work got accepted and appreciated. He wrote the book The Origin of Continents and Oceans in 1915, where it was logically explained, that if you look on the map and put all of the continents together—they all geographically match to create a supercontinent—Pangea. Luckily, he was not discouraged by naysayers, and was very confident in his work—otherwise he could have given up the idea, to avoid any confrontation with skeptics. I am sure, deep inside he knew he was right. If we get some idea—that idea possibly could be good for the humankind, and nothing should discourage us to create it—or publish it. Of course the idea has to be reasonable and then "Time will tell."

5.

Usually, young people think, that they have a lot of time, to fulfill their dreams. Even though, life nowadays is between 50 and 80 years on average, that time somehow passes by very quickly. Sometimes when people get terminally ill, they start thinking about how they have lived their life; and if they have fulfilled their dreams. We don't need to let that happen, and at any stage of the life, we should take a look at our life—and decide if we did enough. Many times, special people left a memorable legacy, when they felt that they could possibly die soon; and created works that we will remember them for forever. Over seven years ago, one particular video on YouTube caught my attention; it was one of the most watched videos that day—named The Last Lecture; the video was a lecture by the Carnegie Mellon University Professor, Randy Pausch, where he gave us a great lesson about what is "Really Achieving Your Childhood Dreams." After watching his video lecture, I was looking forward for his book to be published, and I was one of the first to own it. With his life lessons, he did not touch just his students—he touched all of us. Many, very valuable lessons we have heard from Professor Pausch—but if his video, and book, had not come out, the world would never have heard of him. I mean, his students and family would have known him—but now the whole world has heard of him. Again, leaving legacy is the key; it is the meaning of life.

6.

Just recently—as recent as a few months ago, I came across the Stamford University website for their Medical school; there was an article nicely written by Stamford's neurosurgeon, late Paul Kalanithi. He was a young doctor—that was diagnosed with lung cancer, and he had died from that cancer in March of this year. After reading his beautifully written essay, I looked online, and found his own website—with an introduction to his book When Breath Becomes Air. According to the Sanford Medicine essay, that I read, it looks like it will be a very interesting book, where a young intelligent dying person questions the meaning of life. With the joy of his baby daughter being born, while he was battling cancer; he closed his essay with very touching words: "That message is simple: When you come to one of the many moments in life when you must give an account of yourself, provide a ledger of what you have been, and done, and meant to the world, do not, I pray, discount that you filled a dying man's days with a sated joy, a joy unknown to me in all my prior years, a joy that does not hunger for more and more, but rests, satisfied. In this time, right now, that is an enormous thing." That is exactly what I am talking about when I talk about leaving a legacy. I am very glad, that Mr. Kalanithi had decided to write his book—that will be an excellent legacy of his. I am looking forward to reading it in a few months.

7.

During every war-time many people die, and for many of those poor people, we never learned—that they ever even lived. A young girl, Anne Frank, probably never dreamt of the impact her war diary would have on the world. She wrote it as a personal journal—as a record of the daily activities occurring while being hidden from the Nazi Germans. After the war, it took her father Otto Frank a few attempts to find a publisher, and finally in 1947, he was able to publish it. Today that book is called The Diary of a Young Girl. Her diary was written in a specially modified apartment; where she was hiding—as a Jewish family—they had to be unseen in Amsterdam, during World War II. She was born in Frankfurt, Germany—but when the Nazis came to power her family moved to Amsterdam, The Netherlands. After being in hiding for a long time she still wrote "......I still believe, in spite of everything, that people are really good at heart..," on Saturday, July 15, 1944. Even though, she was just a little girl, Anne had realized the idea, that writing can keep her name alive, even after her death; she could not have known that her daily summary from Wednesday, April 5, 1944 would come true. She wrote that day: "... I want to be useful or bring enjoyment to all people, even those I've never met. I want to go on living even after my death! And that's why I'm so grateful to God for having given me this gift, which I can use to develop myself and to express all that's inside me!..." Well, she did not bring us enjoyment—but definitely gave us all a very important life lesson. Today, it is hard to find a person that has never heard about Anne Frank—this very amazing girl. Just to have you realize how important her writing is—I will mention, that she was titled "Time 100: The Most Important People of the Century," which was published in 1999, by Time magazine.

8.

Anne Frank was very young when she died, and sadly many times people die young. In my personal opinion, if the kids are younger than thirteen they will have a special place in the afterlife—where there will be no hard tasks for them; they will have a lot of play time, and will stay young, possibly eternally. If somebody is older than

thirteen, they should start thinking about leaving a legacy already—
just think of Anne Frank. Write songs, or books, or paint paintings;
create some art, something that at least your family will remember
you—or hopefully the whole world will celebrate you for it. None of us
know how long we will live; every day somebody dies, unexpectedly;
thousands of lives are lost to many different things. Most of the time
accidents are the one to be blamed for, and the person that was killed
could not have done anything about it. Even if we are doing all of the
right things, somehow, we still can be killed or badly injured. If an
accident is not our fault, I am very sure that in the afterlife all things
will settle down, and if there was any unfairness with the help of
Supreme Energy—I have a deep belief that the deceased person will
be awarded properly. Many times, bad things happen to very good
people—as I have mentioned in the Religion part of this book; again
I have a feeling it happens to them because they are too naïve, they
sacrifice themselves too much, to help others—it's possible. We have
to be good to the certain point, but if somebody start abusing us for
being good—we have to stop, and protect ourselves. As I said, there is
also possibility for the other side of the story, when deceased person
looked and acted as a good person from outside, but had very bad, evil
thinking inside—that we were not aware of; those will not be awarded.
We do not know the other side of the story; we are only observers,
but definitely we cannot, and should not, judge anybody. We are not
living anybody else's life, but our own; and have to concentrate only
on our own good doings and thinking in life. Absolutely everyone is
collecting good points for the afterlife on their own—no third parties
involved. We cannot trick Energy, everything is recorded—for sure.

9.

If we did everything right, we do not have to fear death. When we
die, and let's say we get to be judged, again not like the old idea—to
take a seat in front of the old men—and go over all the things, in my

opinion, as I have said before—it is going to be like a scoreboard with the number of points. Of course, if you have a higher number of points you'll end up in a better place. Scoring a higher number of points is possible by doing good deeds, while alive; and I bet you, if you scored a low number of points—you'll immediately regret it. Here is one example—that popped into my head; let's say, there is somebody who has a big business, and constantly is trying to look good in the community—even has donated money sometimes. In their head, they are convinced, that they are good people—but they still can finish life with a low score. Well, there is an explanation for it. When they owned that business, they might have been stealing money—that was intended for workers; at that time, they had probably justified it in their mind, like for example: "Oh, our workers make enough, we will keep this part for us, the workers will never know," and that made their mind peaceful. Remember, Supreme Energy knows everything—absolutely everything. Hence, even if they were donating money, they still had a low number of points in the afterlife. I will put that example to a more obvious case; let's say you own a luxury car transportation company, and you charge your client for driver's gratuity; but decide to keep that gratuity money for your-self, justifying it like: "Oh, we have many other expenses." That explanation is not accepted, because you would still end the year, with a huge profit, even if you gave drivers their gratuity. For absolutely no reason, no one should keep money—that was not intended for them; the client intended that money for the driver, and not for the owner's "other expenses," or extra profit. Few thousands of dollars will not increase the owner's profit much—but those few extra dollars means a lot to the drivers. Owners remember, that most drivers will never ever forgive you for that. You might say: "I didn't do anything illegal," and of course it is not illegal—but like the great Martin Luther King Jr. had said: "Remember what Hitler did in Germany was all legal at the time." If you ask me, I think Hitler ended up with a negative score of points—for sure. We people always have to do the right thing, not only legal—but morally excellent and ethical.

10.

Also as I said in the Religion part of this book, do all things right; also, think and plan in your head, all right things too. Sometimes, death happens so quickly, and we have no time to fix things, which we have messed up on. If we were bad at one part of the life—we still have a chance to change that, while alive—and we have that option to start doing all good things, for the rest of our life—and our regret for being bad has to be honest—from deep inside our soul. Dear God knows if you are honest or fake; we cannot fool Him. Suicide is a bad option, and if you ask me that is the biggest waste of life; and it is the biggest mistake someone can do. We have been gifted a life—to do something important with it; adults know that life is a challenge, and some don't want to try hard; it's definitely not good—and I think the afterlife will be very tough for those who knowingly killed themselves. Life is definitely challenging sometimes, but we have to accept the challenge. Those people that were mentally ill, and did not knowingly commit suicide—are excluded; and their number of points in the afterlife will be determined according to their behavior, before becoming ill. Individuals, who were born mentally ill, will be in a whole separate group if they commit suicide, and should be fine in the afterlife. Just look at the now famous painter Vincent Van Gogh; he was not famous when he committed suicide, but was mentally ill. Before he killed himself, as we all know, he had cut his ear—and at that time somebody should have helped him. Regardless, he continued to work hard, and produced many paintings. His hard work was awarded after he died, because he was a good person— when he was not under the influence of his mental sickness. Now he stands as one of the best artists, which has ever lived on the Earth. Rightfully.

11.

Everyone experiences some hardship during life, as I have never heard of anyone who has lived into adulthood that has not lost somebody, or something they liked. I also have never heard of anyone, who had everything in life run smoothly—there had to be something that bothered them, along the way. People which have survived a war are super cautious about their surroundings—because we have learned a huge life lesson. The price paid for those lessons was very high; we all have scars, somewhere on our brains—that will probably never heal. As I said, I personally still get an unpleasant feeling when I hear fireworks, or even thunder—more than twenty years later. Also, during the war, we get to think about life more—to value it more. When every day is a struggle, we actually, in war-zones, used to worry if we would be alive the next day. Music is art that definitely helps in stressed situation. I remember in April of 1993, right in the middle of the Bosnian War, one amazing lady came to Sarajevo, in person—and with her visit she helped me become stronger. That was Joan Baez, a popular musician—and a lady with a big heart. I heard her when she performed the song Imagine, by John Lennon, with some local music artist; and that made me think of the value of life, it helped me. A simple song that I actually don't agree with all parts now—but back then it was the best life encouragement ever. Thank you Ms. Baez, and Mr. Lennon. Now-days, as I've gotten older, when I need to relax I listen to masterpieces of classical music, created by Wolfgang Amadeus Mozart, Johan Sebastian Bach, Richard Wagner, Antonio Vivaldi, and many more music art geniuses. They all left exceptional legacies with their work, for all of humankind to enjoy.

12.

When hard times arrive in our lives, we always have to think of Victor Hugo's words: "Even the darkest night will end, and the sun will rise," again from the historic novel—Les Miserables. A new day will give us the chance to recuperate, time does not necessarily heal all wounds, but as time passes we get a little bit stronger; and most definitely we always learn a new life-lesson, that will hopefully help us in the future—to be stronger. If we lose hope in our life, that is not good, it is devastating. During the wartime, hope is the most important; and that is when people show their real strength. In the Introduction part of this book, I had mentioned the concentration camp experience of the survivor Victor Frankl. This amazing physiatrist and neurologist observed fellow concentration camp prisoners—and he noticed that every time somebody who has lost the hope for the life—died shortly-after. Or how about the life of Louis (Louie) Zamperini, whose unimaginably tough war experience was told in the book Unbroken by Laura Hillenbrand, and of the same name motion picture by Angelina Jolie. After Mr. Zamperini, and two other fellow Air Force members survived an airplane crash, they were floating on an inflatable raft for many days, out on the Pacific Ocean. One of the unlucky airman, Francis (Mac) McNamara had negative thoughts—and kept on saying "we are gonna die"—and he had died, indeed; Louie and the other airman from their group, Russel (Phil) Phillips, had hope for the life—and had survived the war. True story. Never ever lose hope. Ever.

ACKNOWLEDGEMENTS

In this book I tried to mention most of the stories, and events—which have fascinated me during my life. I want my kids to know about them, and hopefully will learn something from them. I wish my father, peace be upon him, had written me a book—because he had a lot of interesting life experiences. From studying in Belgrade, and London, to running a very successful business—also he was living in several different countries. My father did write me some notes on our family tree, and I am very glad he did that. With this book I am trying to leave my own legacy. I made some conclusions that look right to me. I do not know if I was right—but only time will tell. All which I know, I certainly owe to my life's experience and many great teachers—which have made an influence on me, and on my conclusions. By reading their books, listening to their speeches, and again in a combination with my own life experiences, I was able to put this book together—to leave some sort of legacy behind me. I had to use a lot of data, in the form of numbers, that scientists have calculated, not me, of course. I just calculated small things, like for example, how long it would take to reach the moon at a certain speed. A lot of great authors that are professional scientists, philosophers, and historians have given me distinguished ideas; but then again, I wrote this book that is completely different from any other. This book was written in a very simple, easy to understand style, the same style that I talk to my kids in. I used many resources, and sometimes I used my own conclusions to solve hard understood areas.

My family and me live a very simple family life, and we all—get along very well together, thanks to our positive energy—in a combination with the Universal Energy, of course. Our children, being a high school senior and a high school junior this year, are surprisingly still very attached to us, and we enjoy spending vacations together; very often we go out for family dinners, which I am glad that the kids don't mind. I am very thankful to my dear family for understanding my situation—when I had to work those hundred hour weeks, they were always there for me. I tried to be nice to them too, a few times I would start working at three o'clock in the morning, just to be back by the time they would wake up, and then we would go, all together, to the beach. Those days I counted as my days off.

When I took these 90 days in the summer of 2015 to write this book, I was still working part time—which compared to my old working habits felt very easy. At the end, it took me 55 days which I was actually writing; even though, as I've said before, it took me many years of collecting knowledge—to come up with the conclusion. It is probably good that I did not rush into writing it earlier, because this book would look much different if I wrote it ten years ago. Still, every day I learn something new—and I will try to save ideas that I am getting for the future.

I was raised to always show respect and gratitude to people that have helped me in life. I will use this occasion to say thanks to the people that have helped me on my journey to write this book. As a matter of fact my dear daughter Leila did some of the editing of this book. My family, are the ones that are with me all of the time; not just for this book—but for everything in my life. They are my biggest support; especially my kids who were my inspiration to write this book in the first place, and of course my beautiful wife—who is giving me encouragement at all times. She is a lovely lady, who makes sure that my lunch is ready, every single day—which she cooks on her own, even though she works at school, and has to take care of the house too. Also, she was doing all of the hard work when the kids were little, and she went alone to almost all of the school meetings for our kids, and was helping them with homework too—since I was at work all of the time. Similarly as me growing up, I was attached to my parents and sister; we had the same relationship as I am having now with my family. My father Abduselam (Avdo) died almost nine years ago—and my mom Edinka and my sister Selma don't live nearby me now—but we are in constant touch, through the use of phone and the Internet—pretty much on an everyday basis. They are very dear to me, and their support of whatever I am doing is huge. I love them. From many of my extended family and friends I have felt a lot of kindness. Here I have a chance to mention a few, which are still alive; Azer, Edin and Zlatan Ćiber with their families, Lejla and Lutvo Selimović, Sanjay and Maya Khurana, Aida and Jasmin Ibrahimovic, Suada Alajbegovic, Amela and Emir Čulov, Eldin and Amra Deović, Kip Napier, Romana Miller, Bill Willson, Charles Bloom, Mark Ajmi, Marijana Perić, Siniša and Emina Lubura, Slobodan Stanić, Amela Demirović, Kurlakowsky family, Stelios Pitsillides and Beverly, Dawn Azrak and her family, Jason Jennings, Wendy Crudele, Kevin Lansberry, Jastin Cawthon, Bang Duong and his family, Red McCombs, Jim Abbott, Teresa Filshtein-Sönmez, Christine Tomada, Raymond Watson, Shawna Macnamara, Mustafa Dujso, Vanis Dujso, Kathy Turns, Kerri Ludwig-Kriner, Heidi Ziegler, Megan McFatter and Glen Lee. May your kindness grant you a good everything. Thank You!

REFERENCES

Probably, the most influential individuals on my thinking were ancient time philosophers; but also many contemporary authors wrote very interesting books—thus I have to give them credit for inspiring me. I already tried to include most of the book names and their authors, which gave me best ideas, when I was giving different examples inside of my book—so, hopefully you will be able to read all of them—in case you haven't read those yet. Here I will list more books and websites that gave me the inspiration for making my conclusions, which are not already mentioned in the book. Some of these books I have read multiple times, as they have influenced me in a new way—every time I've read them. Thanks to those authors, and judged by their books, they left a huge legacy—and in the same time they fulfilled their life's meaning, in my opinion. Encyclopedias like Encarta, Britannica, and of course Wikipedia gave me some ideas to, as well as Magazines, like: Scientific American, National Geographic, Smithsonian, Nature, and Science. Also History TV, and Discovery TV is always enjoyment to watch.

Special thanks to these authors, and please read:

- A Short History of Nearly Everything by Bill Bryson,
- The Will to Meaning, by Victor E. Frankl,
- A History of God: The 4000-year Quest of Judaism, Christianity and Islam, by Karen Armstrong,

- Don't Know Much About Bible, by Kenneth C. Davis,

- Don't Know Much About Mythology, by Kenneth C. Davis,

- Guns, Germs, and Steal: The Fates of Human Societies, by Jared Diamond,

- Hyperspace: A Scientific Odyssey Through Parallel Universes, by Michio Kaku,

- Physics of the Impossible: A Scientific Exploration Into the World of Phasers, Force Fields, Teleportation, and Time Travel, by Michio Kaku,

- Blink: The Power of Thinking Without Thinking, by Malcolm Gladwell,

- The Tipping Point: by Malcolm Gladwell,

- The Celestine Prophecy: by James Redfield,

- The Power of Now: by Eckhart Tolle,

- Book of Secrets: Unlocking the Hidden Dimensions of Your Life, by Deepak Chopra,

- You Can Heal Your Life, by Louise L. Hay,

- Art of Happiness at Work, by His Holiness the Dalai Lama and Howard C. Cutler,

- The World Without Us, by Alan Weisman,

- 1491: New Revelations of the Americas Before Columbus,

- Project Orion: The Atomic Spaceship 1957-1965, by George Dyson,

- The God Delusion, by Richard Dawkins,

- Cosmos, by Carl Sagan,

- The Language of God, by Francis S. Collins,

- Biocentrism, by Robert Lanza with Bob Berman,

- You Best Life Now, by Joel Osteen,

- When Bad Things Happen to Good People, by Harold S. Kushner and

- Seabiscuit, by Laura Hillenbrand

Also, many older books you can read for free on:

https://books.google.co.in/books and

https://en.wikisource.org/wiki/Main_Page

My war movie you can find at:

https://www.youtube.com/watch?v=X5uwl1xBZxA

Or, please Google: My War Story - YouTube

In the great age of the Internet, this is where I have gotten many of my notes. I am giving respect, and credit to all of the website owners—for all info.

Please visit these websites:

http://map.gsfc.nasa.gov

http://map.gsfc.nasa.gov/universe/uni_matter.html

http://solarsystem.nasa.gov/planets/beyond

imagine.gsfc.nasa.gov/features/cosmic/nearest_star_info.html

pubs.usgs.gov/gip/geotime/age.html

http://www.independent.co.uk/news/science/35-billionyearold-horribly-smelly-fossil-found-in-australia-is-oldest-ever-complete-example-of-life-on-earth-8940031.html

http://news.discovery.com/earth/plants/874-million-species-on-earth-110823.htm

www.universetoday.com/38125/how-long-have-humans-been-on-earth

www.iucnredlist.org/details/136584/0

earthsky.org/space/milky-way-rotation

https://solarsystem.nasa.gov/planets/sun

http://blackholes.stardate.org/resources/faqs/faq.php?p=sun-become-black-holemnras.oxfordjournals.org/content/448/2/1816.full.pdf coleoguy.github.io/reading.group/Raup_Sepkoski_1982.pdf

www.sciencemag.org/content/261/5119/310

https://www.ncbi.nlm.nih.gov/pmc/articles/PMC2556405

math.ucr.edu/home/baez/extinction

www.iucn.org/?4143/Extinction-crisis-continues-apace

https://www.cbd.int/convention/guide

iss.astroviewer.net/

www.nasa.gov/mission_pages/station/main/index.html

www.theguardian.com/science/2010/oct/24/international-space-station-nasa-astronauts

https://solarsystem.nasa.gov/planets/moon

www.nasa.gov/sites/default/files/files/Distance_to_the_Moon.pdf

www.history.com/topics/black-death

https://virus.stanford.edu/uda

www.overpopulation.org/

www.worldometers.info/world-population/india-population

www.livescience.com/50414-chicxulub-crater-drilling.html

neo.jpl.nasa.gov/images/yucatan.html

www.universetoday.com/107791/will-the-sun-explode

www.space.com/23475-proxima-centauri-hubble-telescope-photo.html

www.universetoday.com/15403/how-long-would-it-take-to-travel-to-the-nearest-star

physics.nist.gov/cgi-bin/cuu/Value?c

voyager.jpl.nasa.gov/mission/didyouknow.html

earthsky.org/space/alpha-centauri-travel-time

www.space.com/11337-human-spaceflight-records-50th-anniversary.html

http://www.realclearscience.com/blog/2014/04/interstellar_travel.html

www.oriondrive.com/p1_story_history.php

ntrs.nasa.gov/archive/nasa/casi.ntrs.nasa.gov/19760065935.pdf

news.discovery.com/space/history-of-space/project-daedalus-size-comparison-110119.htm

www.nvahof.org/hof/hof-2012/robert-w-bussard

scribol.com/anthropology-and-history/what-the-lascaux-cave-paintings-tell-us-about-how-our-ancestors-understood-the-stars

www.metmuseum.org/toah/hd/chav/hd_chav.htm

toba.arch.ox.ac.uk/

www.lllf.uam.es/~clase/acceso_local/LgCapabili.pdf

www.historian.net/hxwrite.htm

www.amnh.org/

www.ies.sas.ac.uk/library/ies-collections/museum-writing

www.metmuseum.org/toah/hd/wrtg/hd_wrtg.htm

www.britishmuseum.org/explore/themes/writing/historic_writing.aspx

www.ancientscripts.com/ws_types.html

www.omniglot.com/writing/types.htm

etcsl.orinst.ox.ac.uk/section5/tr535.htm

http://www.smithsonianmag.com/science-nature/ten-ancient-stories-and-geological-events-may-have-inspired-them-180950347/?utm_source=facebook.com&utm_medium=socialmedia&utm_campaign=04042014&utm_content=sciencemythgeology

www.sparknotes.com/lit/gilgamesh

factsanddetails.com/world/cat56/sub363/item1525.html

avalon.law.yale.edu/ancient/hamframe.asp

www.ushistory.org/civ/4c.asp

ancienthistory.about.com/od/indusvalleyciv/a/harappanculture.htm

www.uio.no/studier/emner/hf/iakh/HIS2172/h06/undervisningsmateriale/harappa.doc

www.ancient.eu/Indus_Valley_Civilization

https://www.sscnet.ucla.edu/southasia/History/Ancient/Indus2.html

www.britannica.com/topic/Indus-civilization

www.ancientscripts.com/brahmi.html

www.omniglot.com/writing/brahmi.htm

www.omniglot.com/writing/sanskrit.htm

www.britannica.com/topic/Sanskrit-language

www.sacred-texts.com/hin/maha

www.britannica.com/topic/Mahabharata

www.sacred-texts.com/hin/gita

www.bhagavad-gita.org/

www.sacred-texts.com/hin/rama

valmikiramayan.net/

www.sacred-texts.com/hin

www.ancient.eu/The_Vedas

www.religionfacts.com/vedas

ced.ochs.org.uk/courses/vedas-andupanishadsgclid=CjwKEA
jw67SvBRC1m5zPv4GboAUSJAB6MJlkRTqnp_bXADk5o
IO9leJiTgKEYw-GQdmm8FR7ZQjUnhoCCPjw_wcB

www.biography.com/people/buddha-9230587

www.britannica.com/biography/Maha-Maya

buddhism.about.com/od/lifeofthebuddha/a/buddhalife.htm

www.buddhanet.net/e-learning/buddhism/lifebuddha/1lbud.htm

www.britannica.com/topic/nirvana-religion

dictionary.reference.com/browse/papyrus

www.sacred-texts.com/egy/ebod

www.britishmuseum.org/explore/highlights/highlight_objects/aes/t/the_rosetta_stone.aspx

www.britishmuseum.org/explore/highlights/highlight_objects/aes/p/book_of_the_dead_of_ani.aspx

www.ancientegypt.co.uk/writing/rosetta.html

www.historyrocket.com/age-of-history/bronze-age/Bronze-Age-Writing-Systems.html

www.ancient.eu/Bronze_Age

www.ancientscripts.com/chinese.html

ancienthistory.about.com/od/writing/qt/033009chinesescrpt.htm

www.britishmuseum.org/explore/themes/writing/historic_writing.aspx

science.nationalgeographic.com/science/archaeology/emperor-qin

www.smithsonianmag.com/history/terra-cotta-soldiers-on-the-march-30942673

www.britannica.com/topic/Mesoamerican-civilization

study.com/academy/lesson/mesoamerican-civilizations-the-olmecs-to-cortes.html

www.ancientscripts.com/maya.html

whc.unesco.org/en/tentativelists/5739

www.ancient-origins.net/ancient-places-europe/do-tartaria-tablets-contain-evidence-earliest-known-writing-system-002103

www.omniglot.com/writing/vinca.htm

www.ancient-origins.net/ancient-places-europe/danube-valley-civilisation-script-oldest-writing-world-001343

www.ancient-wisdom.com/serbiavinca.htm

news.bbc.co.uk/2/hi/science/nature/2956925.stm

www.ancient-symbols.com/symbols-directory/jiahu.html

www.ancientscripts.com/cretan_hieroglyphs.html

people.ku.edu/~jyounger/Hiero

www.self.gutenberg.org/articles/cretan_hieroglyphs

www.ancientscripts.com/lineara.html

www.omniglot.com/writing/lineara.htm

people.ku.edu/~jyounger/LinearA

www.ancientscripts.com/linearb.html

www.omniglot.com/writing/linearb.htm

www.britishmuseum.org/explore/highlights/highlight_objects/
gr/c/tablets_with_linear_b_script.aspx

whc.unesco.org/en/list/849

www.history.com/topics/ancient-history/trojan-war

www.classics.upenn.edu/myth/php/homer/index.php?page=trojan

study.com/academy/lesson/the-iliad-the-odyssey-summary-
characters.html

www.webpages.uidaho.edu/engl257/ancient/iliad_and_
odyssey.htm

www.baruch.cuny.edu/library/alumni/online_exhibits/
digital/2000/c_n_c/c_01_epic/backgrounds.htm

ngm.nationalgeographic.com/features/world/asia/lebanon/
phoenicians-text.html

www.history.com/news/ask-history/why-is-a-marathon-26-2-miles

www.britannica.com/biography/Herodotus-Greek-historian

www.history.com/topics/ancient-history/herodotus

www.biography.com/people/socrates-9488126

plato.stanford.edu/entries/socrates

www.philosophypages.com/ph/plat.htm

www.ucmp.berkeley.edu/history/aristotle.html

www.history.com/topics/ancient-history/aristotle

www.omniglot.com/writing/etruscan.htm

www.britannica.com/topic/ancient-Italic-people

www.omniglot.com/writing/latin2.htm

www.ushistory.org/civ/6a.asp

www.britannica.com/place/Roman-Republic

www.livescience.com/45510-anno-domini.html

www.telegraph.co.uk/news/worldnews/the-pope/9693576/Jesus-was-born-years-earlier-than-thought-claims-Pope.html

www.livescience.com/3482-jesus-man.html

www.biography.com/people/jesus-christ-9354382

www.teslasociety.com/biography.htm

www.history.com/topics/inventions/nikola-tesla

www.smithsonianmag.com/history/the-rise-and-fall-of-nikola-tesla-and-his-tower-11074324

www.cnn.com/2010/US/02/19/tiger.woods.transcript

indiatoday.intoday.in/education/story/dashrath-manjhi/1/451471.html

https://in.news.yahoo.com/man-moved-mountain-000000051.html

www.charlotteobserver.com/news/local/article22753806.html

www.theguardian.com/sport/2015/jun/01/harriette-thompson-92-oldest-woman-complete-marathon-san-diego

www.irenasendler.org/

www.auschwitz.dk/sendler.htm

www.cnn.com/2015/06/09/health/james-harrison-golden-arm-blood-rhesus

www.huffingtonpost.com/2015/06/09/james-harrison-blood-donor_n_7546026.html

tzg-krapina.hr/en/museum_of_early_man

www.britannica.com/topic/polytheism

plato.stanford.edu/entries/pantheism

www.britannica.com/topic/monotheism

plato.stanford.edu/entries/monotheism

buddhism.about.com/od/buddha/a/birthofbuddha.htm

www.stanna.at/content.php?p=1&lang=de

https://www.usconstitution.net/const.pdf

www.nobelprize.org/nobel_prizes/peace/laureates/1979/teresa-lecture.html

www.britannica.com/biography/Mother-Teresa

www.deism.com/deism.htm

www.britannica.com/topic/Deism

web.randi.org/

www.americanmuseumofmagic.org/

https://en.wikipedia.org/wiki/Jean_Eugène_Robert-Houdin

http://americanhumanist.org/Humanism/Humanist_Manifesto_I

www.hope-of-israel.org/cmas1.htm

dictionary.reference.com/browse/wealth?s=t

www.si.edu/about

siarchives.si.edu/history/exhibits/stories/last-will-and-testament-october-23-1826

newsdesk.si.edu/factsheets/founding-smithsonian-institution

www.forbes.com/billionaires

www.forbes.com/profile/bill-gates?list=billionaires

www.gatesnotes.com/

www.gatesfoundation.org/Who-We-Are

www.forbes.com/sites/matthewherper/2011/11/02/the-second-coming-of-bill-gates

https://www.ted.com/talks/bill_and_melinda_gates_why_giving_
away_our_wealth_has_been_the_most_satisfying_thing_we_
ve_done?language=en#t-1545142

http://www.investopedia.com/university/greatest/warrenbuffett.asp

www.biography.com/people/warren-buffett-9230729

www.forbes.com/profile/warren-buffett

givingpledge.org/

money.cnn.com/2015/06/02/news/companies/giving-pledge-
billionaires-buffett-gates

www.imdb.com/title/tt1183919

www.bobmarley.com/history

www.nba.com/history/legends/drazen-petrovic/index.html

www.halloffame.fiba.com/pages/eng/hof/indu/p/lid_9024_
newsid/18013/playBio.html

http://www.cnn.com/2009/HEALTH/04/20/hawking.als/index.
html?iref=24hours

http://www.scientificamerican.com/article/stephen-hawking-als/

www.jimabbott.net/

http://www.lifewithoutlimbs.org/about-nick/bio

http://www.wordsofjoy.com/James_Brown_BIO.htm

https://www.cia.gov/library/publications/resources/the-world-factbook/

http://www.nlm.nih.gov

www.who.int/en

http://www.nobelprize.org/nobel_prizes/medicine/laureates/1931/

http://healingtools.tripod.com/primecause1.html/primecause2.html

https://www.conncoll.edu/news/news-archive/2013/student-
faculty-research-suggests-oreos-can-be-compared-to-drugs-of-
abuse-in-lab-rats.html#.VfBPbkr3arX

http://www.getsmartaboutdrugs.com/drugs/heroin

https://en.wikisource.org/wiki/Aphorisms

www.cmu.edu/randyslecture/book/index.html

http://stanmed.stanford.edu/2015spring/before-i-go.html

http://paulkalanithi.com/book/

http://articles.orlandosentinel.com/1993-04-16/news/9304160594_
1_joan-baez-sarajevo-singer-joan